Modern churches of the world

Designed by Gillian Greenwood

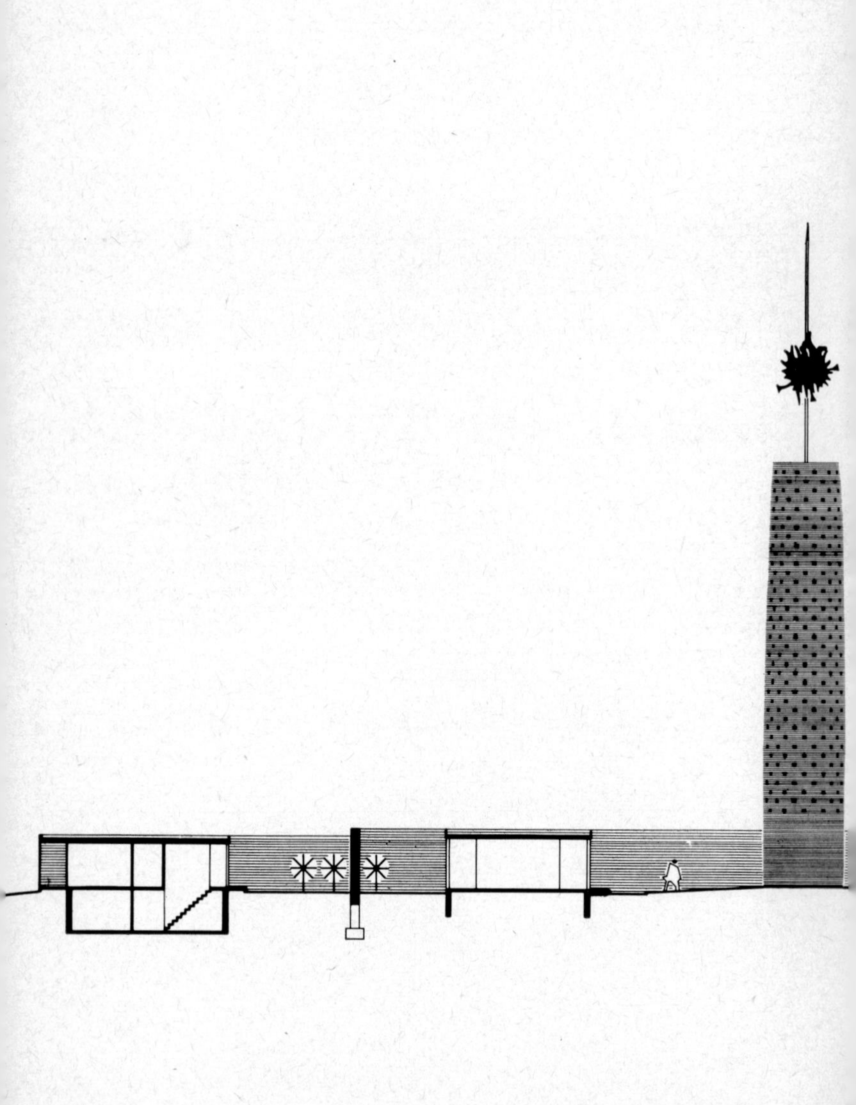

Robert Maguire and Keith Murray

MODERN CHURCHES
OF THE WORLD

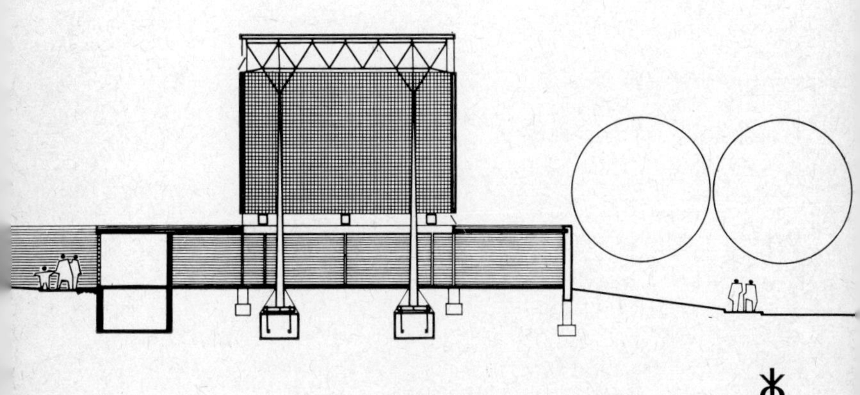

a dutton vista pictureback
General editor David Herbert

Published in London by Studio Vista Limited
Blue Star House, Highgate Hill, N 19
and in New York by E. P. Dutton and Co Inc
201 Park Avenue South, New York 3, NY
Set in 8pt Univers 2pts leaded
Made and printed in Great Britain by
Richard Clay (The Chaucer Press) Ltd, Bungay, Suffolk

Contents

Acknowledgements

The Authors and Publishers would like to express their thanks to Dipl.-Ing. Frau Maria Schwarz for her help and to the following who supplied photographs. (References are to page numbers.)

Architectural Review 92 (top)
Ateljé Sundahe 141
Vincent Bockstieger 157 (top)
Gisela Buddeberg 136
J. Caps 53
George H. Cardozo 126
Caroën 60–1
Casali 98, 99 (top and bottom), 100 (top), 101
George Cserna 127, 128 (bottom), 129, 130 (bottom), 131
Theo Felten 12, 37, 116
G. Forrest Wilson 144–5, 146 (bottom)
Friebel 42 (bottom)
Norman Gold 13, 90–1, 93
Y. Guillemaut 17 (bottom)
Lucien Hervé 49, 50 (top), 51 (top and bottom), 54 (top and bottom), 55
F. Hubmann 75
Richard Hughes 120, 122 (top and bottom)
René Jacques 62 (bottom)
G. E. Kidder Smith 85 (top)
André Le Donné 63, 65
Lorenz 152
John McCann 108–9
Museum of Finnish Architecture 105–7
Gösta Nordin 140
Artur Pfau-Foto 25, 58 (top), 59 (top and bottom), 82–3, 85 (bottom), 87, 89 (top and bottom), 113–14, 115 (top), 117, 119
Pietinem 70, 71 (top and bottom), 72 (bottom), 73
Photo-Anker 79, 81 (top and bottom)
Publicam 132–4, 135 (bottom)
Radio Times Hulton Picture Library 8
Renger-Patsch 23, 24 (left and right)
Rheinisches Bildarchiv 38, 40
Inge v.d. Ropp 150–1
H. Schmidt-Glassner 26
H. Schmölz 95
Schmölz & Ullrich 11, 30–1, 33 (top and bottom), 34–5, 56–7, 66–8, 69 (bottom), 94, 96 (bottom), 97
H. H. Schnell 139
Rainer Senn 102 (top), 103–4
James R. Smith 123–4, 125 (bottom)
Sport and General Press Agency Ltd 111
Heinz von Sterneck 143
Hugh N. Stratford 147, 149
Gustl Tögel 78
Wilhein Wagner 74
Michael Wolgensinger 44–5, 47 (top and bottom)

Introduction

Like all the other material things the Christian Church uses, church buildings are not essential to the Church's life.[1] If this is forgotten churches quickly become an end in themselves, a danger to the life they should serve. Yet the Church uses material things; especially those things which are apt because of their intrinsic symbolic significance. The bread and wine which Christ chose to use in the Last Supper already had a deep meaningfulness, to which he gave a new dimension in the context of thanksgiving. When the Salvation Army forms a circle on a windy street corner

it also uses a form with deep-rooted meaning. A *place* is made by the circle of people (where before there was only placelessness) for the time of the service; a *centre* is created. In the very simplest form a church is built.

In a de-Christianized industrial area such a church may be the best for the situation. The Celtic missionaries to the Anglo-Saxons of the seventh century set up a cross and gathered the people round it. When a family arranges a room for the 'house church' to meet, setting the table symmetrically in the place which seems most right, it again builds a church. In each case simple but symbolic means are used to make a place for the Church to meet for worship. The church building is an extension of this.

But what distinguishes a church from a circle of people or an arranged kitchen is that where these *set apart* a place for a short time, a church is permanently set apart for worship. The act of

[1] 'Since, Lord, once again . . . in the steppes of Asia, I have neither bread nor wine nor altar, I will raise myself above these symbols up to the pure majesty of Reality, and I, your priest, will offer You, upon the altar of the Whole Earth, the labour and the suffering of the world.' *Pierre Teilhard de Chardin*

setting apart a church is similar to the setting apart of Sunday, a symbolic act, using symbolic means, to help man to meet God. Inevitably, once a place is set apart, it takes on a special character by virtue of this symbolic act, a character not entirely unique to Christianity (as bread and wine are not unique to Christianity) yet transformed for the particular purpose of the Church–the character possessed by set apart places since the earliest human prehistory.[1] The architectural means by which such places have been distinguished show great variety, yet follow certain patterns: the single stone, the bethel, the Celtic missionary's cross, the enclosing circle made by ditches, earthworks, stones (or people in the case of the Salvation Army) and the mound or holy hill, either natural or 'made'.

These patterns, which use the symbolic means of architecture, are essentially concerned with the creation of places for meeting. The Roman Catholic church and the Friends' Meeting House have this in common: they are both built as places of meeting, between man and man and between men and God. The Roman Catholic rite for the consecration of a church uses Genesis 28.17: 'How dreadful is this place! This is none other but the house of God, and this is the gate of heaven'—Jacob's words after his dream of the ladder with angels going up and down, expressing communication between God and man. Jacob set up a stone and promised that if he returned safely 'this stone which I have set for a pillar shall be God's house'. The use of the word *sanctuary* is expressive of this idea, and while it has also become the name of a part of a church, it extends to the whole place and is indeed used in this sense by some Christian groups.[2]

Once a building has been set apart for worship it acquires these meanings; as with the bread and wine, they are inherent. If the meanings are not made manifest in the architecture, then the symbolic means of architecture will be 'speaking' of something different, and there will be a conflict, an implied negation. If these meanings are not accepted, then the only way to avoid the conflict is not to have churches. Churches cost a lot of money; the expense is only justified if one believes that the building in all its implications can and should be creative in the life of the Church. Otherwise it would be better to use the school hall or any other kind of building not set apart.

[1] Studies in comparative religion show the distribution throughout the world of the symbolic 'set-apart place' and the 'centre'. See Mircea Eliade: *Patterns in Comparative Religion*, Sheed and Ward, London, 1958.

[2] In our commentaries on the churches in this book we have sometimes used the word 'sanctuary' in its narrower sense to describe the area around the altar or communion table, since this is traditional and generally understood. We have also used the phrase 'altar-place', which is clumsy, but which we prefer. The common German term is *altarplatz*.

We have chosen the buildings in this book for their architectural quality, and by this we do *not* mean their quality as self-sufficient works of art. Architectural quality is *aptness* at all levels–a 'nearness to need', an appropriate *place* for the activity the building houses (which it houses so well that it becomes a symbol of that activity, of that aspect of man) ; and a relevance to its environment and the kind of culture of which it is the product, down to the kind of stuff it is made of and the way the stuff is used.

From what we have said above, it will be obvious that our choice includes only those buildings which show in some way or other those meanings which we see in the very idea of a church. Yet the ways are very diverse, and the criterion of aptness leads to a most heterogeneous collection, as varied as the human situations which have given rise to the buildings. There is no typical modern church.

The notion of architecture 'speaking' of this or that should not be confused with the use of literary symbols, as for instance in a certain church built in the shape of alpha and omega (and comprehensible only from a helicopter) or another church whose roof is built 'to symbolize' praying hands. Such devices depend on translation into an intellectual concept—the building needs to be *explained* by an idea which is extraneous to it as a building. Architecture does not need to be explained : it is a manifestation, understood at a simple, fundamental level of consciousness. Its effect can be either positive or negative.

In the sixth-century font at Kélibia form and meaning are interwoven in a way which no modern example has achieved. Even when empty the rounded wateriness of its forms and the fluidity

Font at Kélibia

of its mosaic convey the preformal and potential nature of the life-giving water; and the cruciform depression which seems to be continuously evolving from it underlines those further meanings, concerned with death and burial, life and resurrection, which water has always had and which have been given new significance by the Church in baptism.[1] But while one may point out these facts the object itself seems so much more articulate.

Notice, however, that the font at Kélibia 'speaks' about baptism by concerning itself with water; by, as it were, surrendering itself to the nature of the water which is the main carrier of meaning. It does not itself attempt to do what the water can do through its essential nature; but is simply—though brilliantly—a context for the water.

Baptistery at St Albert, Saarbrücken

The baptistery at St Albert, Saarbrücken, is also a context for water; a well-like circular space in which the font is a running fountain. The circular shape is complementary to its function, as also is the use of stone for the floor and font. One could produce a rational justification for this statement, but it is made unnecessary by the vast history of association between water and the circular form and the material stone. Compare the Round Church at Essen (p. 26) which curiously has the character of a huge baptistery, so emphatically that this prevents its becoming convincing as a church.

[1] 'It (baptism) represents death and burial, life and resurrection. . . . When we plunge our head in water as in a tomb, the old man is immersed, wholly buried; when we come out of the water the new man appears at that moment.' *St John Chrysostom*

St Christophorus, Cologne-Niehl

In St Christophorus at Cologne-Niehl, the font is set in the space of the church, not in a separate baptistery, in order to make manifest the relationship between baptism and the Thanksgiving.[1] This is achieved through a physical relationship in the organized space of the building between the place of the font and the place of the altar, by having the Easter candle permanently by the font, and by the forms and material of font and altar. They are of the same stone, but the square formal blockness of the altar contrasts with the low hollowed-out circularity of the font; each says something, the one about meeting and sacrifice, the other about baptism.

The font at St Paul, Bow Common, is made from a hemispherical industrial stoneware vat set in an octagonal concrete block. It stands inside the inner door, and is the first thing encountered after one has passed through the porch into the church. From the

[1] Thanksgiving (a translation of Eucharist) : Mass, Lord's Supper, Communion Service.

low-ceilinged, comparatively dark place where it stands, the church beyond increases in light and expands itself in light-containing space. Again by spatial relationship something is said about baptism, the rite of transition from darkness to light. The font is only a context for water; through the reflection of the light beyond on the surface of the deep round pool, the wateriness of the water is made more apparent.

These examples of fonts demonstrate architectural means, and none of them resort to tricks or illusion: the means themselves stand as realities. The baptistery of the church at Baranzate (p. 98) is at the entrance to the church; one descends to it and mounts again into the church on the other side, an arrangement which in itself is architecturally apt. But from outside the door, a pool of running water is reflected in the plateglass window of the baptistery, giving the impression that the font inside is standing in the living water: a clever trick but hollow as soon as it is seen for what it is.

Most of the churches chosen for this book are the results of the conjunction of two movements, the Liturgical Movement in the Church and the Modern Movement in architecture. Both have their roots in the nineteenth century, and although by the time they appeared as recognizable movements in the present century

Font at St Paul, Bow Common, London

they seemed to have no connection, some of the roots were common to both.

The Liturgical Movement has rediscovered the essential creative significance of the liturgy as the source of renewal of the life and teaching of the Church. This reformation is having its influence over a wide spectrum of the Church—at an Ecumenical Liturgical Conference held at Swanwick in 1961 there was a surprising measure of agreement among contributors, who included Orthodox, Roman Catholics, Anglicans, Presbyterians, Methodists, Baptists, Lutherans and Calvinists.

The social function of architecture was a constant theme of most of the founders of the Modern Movement in architecture; it reversed the generally accepted nineteenth-century concept of architecture as an art in which style is paramount. Dr Reyner Banham has shown[1] how, at the beginning of the Modern Movement, architecture was once again seen to have a symbolic role in society.

Both these principles bear a direct relationship of descent from the realization, in the middle of the nineteenth century, that liturgy and architecture have a functional relationship—an insight which, however quaint the tone of its apologetics may make it seem to us now, had such far-reaching effects on architecture beyond the Church that it is surprising that the Church had forgotten about it by the end of the century.

In our own century the Liturgical Movement has shown again the intimate connection between liturgy and architecture. Without this connection, new churches could be only superficially modern in style, completely lacking the essential character of the architecture of the Modern Movement. A church like St Laurentius at Munich-Gern (p. 78), though apparently traditional in style, is more essentially a product of the Modern Movement than a great number of new churches which are decked out with 'exciting' modern forms, but are not fundamentally concerned with the needs of the developing liturgical life of a Christian community. The first really great building arising from the meeting of the two movements was Corpus Christi at Aachen (p. 22) by the architect Rudolf Schwarz: Schwarz was closely in touch with a great theologian of the Liturgical Movement, Romano Guardini.

When architecture becomes a matter of style, the relationship between client and architect is of little consequence. But once the architect recognizes that a building fulfills a practical and symbolic function in the life of a community then this relationship becomes crucial. The architect must get in touch with the life he serves.

[1] Reyner Banham: *Theory and Design in the First Machine Age*, Architectural Press, London, 1960.

Auguste Perret
NOTRE-DAME DU RAINCY RC
PARIS · FRANCE 1922–23

Reinforced concrete was invented early in the nineteenth century. At first it was used mostly for civil engineering. Although this was not the first concrete church, generally where concrete had been used in building it was considered too crude to be seen. In 1922 when Perret designed, engineered and built Notre-Dame du Raincy, it was a shock—a large church (for 2,000) built in this crude material.

Steel was also considered crude, and a few years later in the Steel Church (p. 18) Otto Bartning did for steel what Perret did for concrete; both showed the fineness of the material when it was used according to its own nature. Both churches in their different ways are stripped down and sinewy, beautiful in the way a greyhound is beautiful. In both buildings there is a clear relation between the inside and the outside: the enclosing wall is taut, as though the church were slightly pressurized.

At Le Raincy the columns stand within the space, the glass and concrete wall wraps round freely, the vaulting springs smoothly from beams above the columns. The extraordinary tower, made up of columns thrusting up through the church, is crazy but magnificent. Although the walls, columns and vault are all made of con-

Notre-Dame du Raincy

crete, the way concrete is used in each is quite distinct, as though it were three different but related materials. Part of the genius of the building is Perret's recognition of these distinctions and the feeling with which he used them.

The church is important not only because it showed how concrete could be used for churches, but because it was a real development liturgically. Although the plan looks fairly conventional, the space of the building is quite unlike that of a Gothic revival building or an early Christian basilica. In Notre-Dame du Raincy one can begin to feel new life in liturgy as well as new life in architecture.

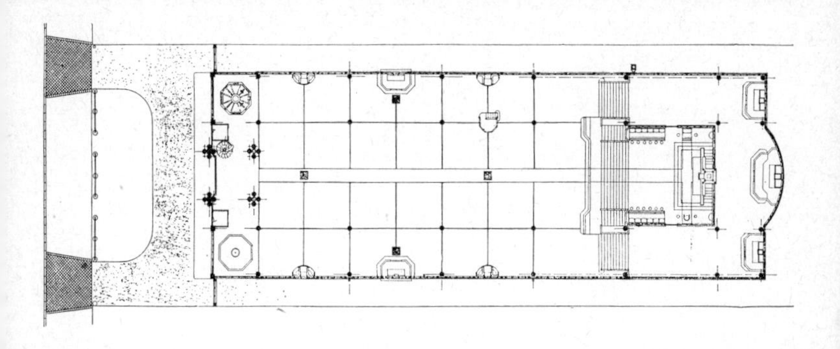

Notre-Dame du Raincy

Otto Bartning
THE STEEL CHURCH Evangelical
ESSEN · WEST GERMANY 1928

The Steel Church was originally erected for the Pressa ausstellung in Cologne in 1928. After the exhibition closed, it was taken down and re-erected at Essen, where it remained until bombed in 1943. It was built with steel given by manufacturers. Though rolled steel sections had been used before in churches, they had nearly always been disguised with stone or concrete. Here the frame was completely exposed. The stained glass was fixed directly into the steel frame and where opaque walls were needed, panels consisting of wood on the inside, insulating material, and copper sheeting on the outside were used. These were also fixed directly into the steel.

At Le Raincy (p. 15) Perret showed what concrete could do. Bartning did the same for steel in this church, and no church since has approached it in its radical use of a material. Comparable secular buildings are Mies van der Rohe's Lakeshore Drive apartments, Chicago, or Peter and Alison Smithson's school at Hunstanton.

Like many of the best buildings of the twenties and thirties the church had an uncompromising and slightly inhuman quality, but it was wholly appropriate to the place for which it was built. This shows clearly if one compares it to the church at Rohrbach by Von Branca (p. 136), which is also appropriate in its country setting. The Steel Church spoke out clearly in an industrial area, where the

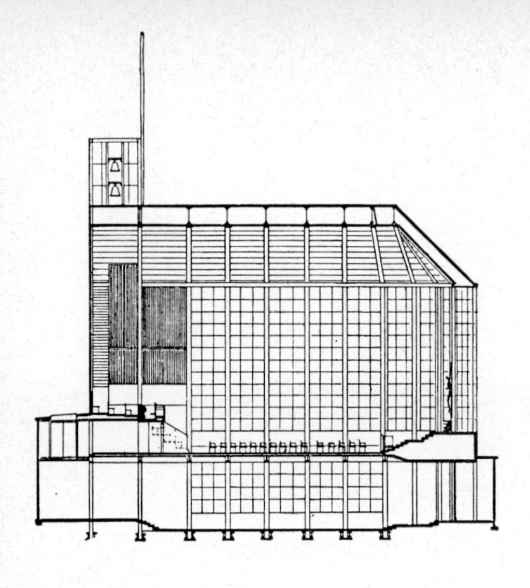

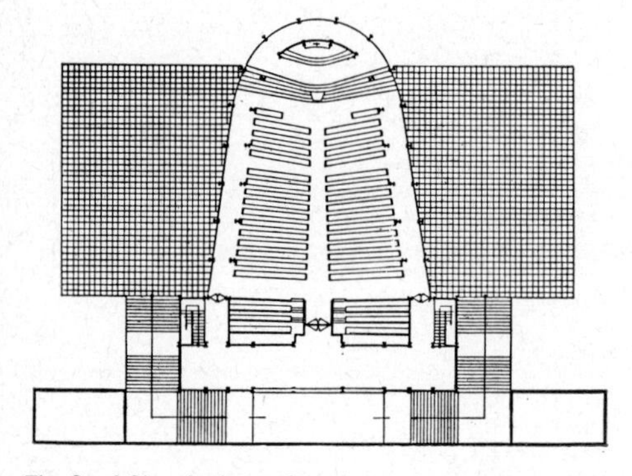

The Steel Church plan and section

country church would have looked like a goose in a smelting shop.

In early projects, and in the design of the Round Church (p. 26) built just after this, Bartning is clearly concerned with a unified, uniting space. In the Steel Church the nave and the sanctuary have been drawn together with a taut loop, which ties in the space. The Steel Church had a dramatically raised sanctuary, but the unity of the space prevented this becoming dissociated. The church floor was raised above ground level; below it there was a hall. The entrance sequence into the church emphasized the idea of going up into 'the place between heaven and earth'.

It is especially sad that it was bombed, as there are few churches so completely of its time.

Rudolf Schwarz
CORPUS CHRISTI RC
AACHEN · WEST GERMANY 1928–30

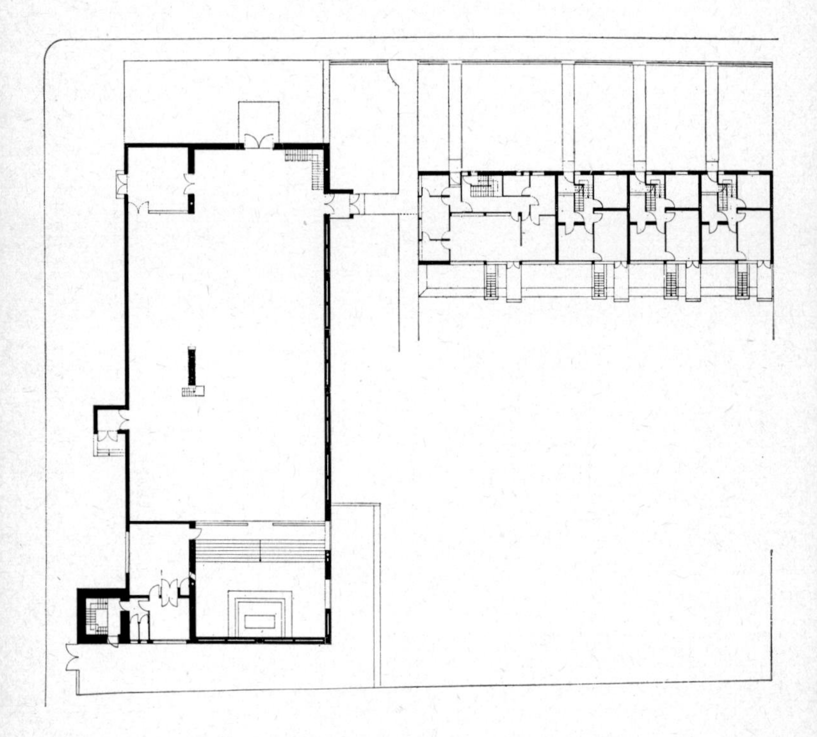

It is difficult to see why Schwarz's first church did not become a classic illustration of the 'old modern architecture' of the 1930s. It has all the qualifying attributes: the purity of form, the crisp white unbroken surfaces, the affinities with certain industrial products which were seen as typifying the new age, and a quality as large-scale sculpture which surpasses much that was given greater applause at the time. It also has an intensity of feeling which is more specifically religious, and it may be that this attribute was too much for the architectural rationalists to take; just as its severity was too much for many churchmen, who referred to it as 'the factory'.

It is difficult to overestimate its effect on the subsequent development of church-building. For it was not only the first major entry of

Corpus Christi

Corpus Christi

Roman Catholic church-building into a new world of architectural ideas. It was also the outcome of another world of ideas, those of the movement for liturgical renewal in the Roman Catholic Church, which received its greatest impetus in Germany; Schwarz was in close touch with the theologians of the movement. The church is therefore at once the fruit of a developed understanding of liturgy and an expression of this in terms of a fresh, vital architecture. The building derives its vigour from the conviction and stature of its architect in both fields.

Schwarz acknowledged a great debt to Romano Guardini, with whom he was close friends and who collaborated with him on actual projects. At Aachen he was greatly influenced by the theologian's thought on the meaningfulness of emptiness, and has written that if the limitations of architectural expression are not recognized, then the architecture may fail through trying to say something that it cannot. He deliberately simplified the building so that the emptiness could be filled by that which only the holy can make meaningful.

Otto Bartning
THE ROUND CHURCH Evangelical
ESSEN · WEST GERMANY 1929–30

Otto Bartning, like Dominikus Böhm, was interested in circular plans for churches during the 1920s. He built this church a little earlier than Böhm's St Engelbert at Cologne (p. 34). The plan is based on a project of 1922. The church is in the shape of a great rotunda which has the advantage and dangerous appeal of a clear symbolic form. Outside it is magnificent, with an intense bony severity; inside the function has been shoe-horned into the plan-form. Right at the beginning of the freer development of modern church design, this church demonstrated the fallacy of the circular plan with an altar-table near the centre. Because of its form there is an intense concentration at the geometrical centre, which is actually where the font is. In spite of the table, organ and galleries pushed into the space, and in spite of the small size of the font, its place at the centre of the powerful circular form of the

The Round Church

building makes the place into a great baptistery, with the other things added; in 1927 Bartning did a superb baptistery for the Kunstausstellung at Berlin where the natural relationship between the circular plan and the font were beautifully shown.

A comparison of these two buildings, the Round Church and the Berlin baptistery, is fascinating, because it illustrates the relationship between function and the symbolic form of a building. Circles and water are related because containers are circular, whether cup, bowl, barrel, womb or font, and because circles are part of a complex symbolic structure including baptism in which water is the key (see Mircea Eliade: *Patterns in Comparative Religion: Waters and water symbolism*). On the other hand, altars and tables are square rather than circular.

Even though the planning may be misguided, the interior has the life, and guts which distinguish Bartning's work.

The Round Church plan and section

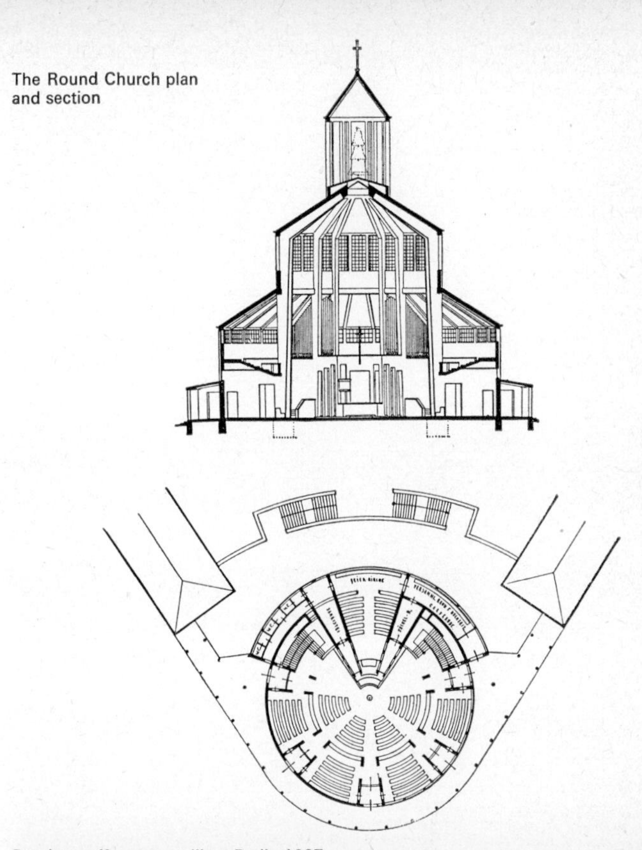

Baptistery, Kunstausstelling, Berlin 1927

Dominikus Böhm
CHURCH AT NORDERNEY RC
WEST GERMANY 1930

Designed at about the same time as Böhm's St Engelbert at Cologne (p. 34), this church is radically different in every respect, except in Böhm's constant concern for the part of the people in the Church's worship. Norderney shows new developments on two fronts: a more human scale than the grand manner of his earlier projects, which in St Engelbert still threatens to separate the congregation from the liturgical action; and the now direct influence of the new architecture of the time, which result in his suddenly stripping away the historical motifs with which he had previously made play—often with irrelevant effect—and allow him to produce a building at once intimate and monumental.

The church has obvious affinities with Rudolf Schwarz's church at Aachen (p. 22), of the same year. In general organization: the single low side-aisle, with minimum columns, contrasted with the

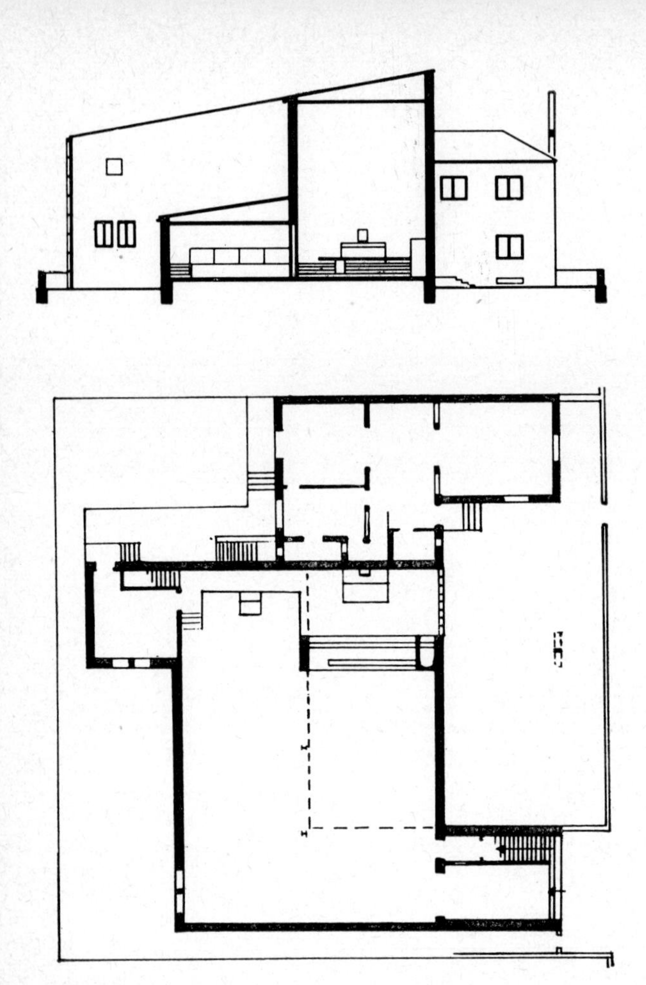

Church at Norderney plan and section

height of the main space yet comparable in area; in numerous smaller details; and in the first real breath of fresh air from the new architecture, hitherto ignored by the Church. Schwarz had worked in Böhm's office until shortly before; both men were well in touch with each other and, more significantly, with the springs of the Liturgical Movement in Germany.

Dominikus Böhm
ST ENGELBERT RC
COLOGNE-RIEHL · WEST GERMANY 1930–32

This church is historically important as the first Catholic church of modern times to break away from the rectangular plan. Though few modern circular churches really work, St Engelbert had a liberating effect, making other developments possible at a time when church design was rigid.

The main entrance to the church from the street is up a wide flight of steps and through doors under the organ-gallery. There is another way in, which is commonly used, past the baptistery, through a chapel and up steps into the church. This gives the feeling that the church is a high place; without being dramatic, this entrance sequence is strangely impressive. The circular form of the nave and the related altar-space give a sense of 'placeness' which unites the congregation and the 'place of the altar', even though the flight of steps up to the altar and the dramatic side-lighting make the altar-place stagy. The curved seating is fixed

and rigid, but it is so played down that it does not dominate the space, as fixed seating is apt to. The pulpit is well related to the congregation, but the ringing bathroom acoustics in the building make loudspeakers necessary. This acoustic character is not good for preaching, but it must be fine for singing.

The interior of the building is taut and calm, but the shape, and the way that the white plaster and the exotic marble of the altar have been used, create a slight feeling of floating unreality; the same kinds of material have a quite different effect in the church built at about the same time by Rudolf Schwarz at Aachen (p. 22).

The outside of the church is strong, but there is also something disturbing about its scale, which seems to suggest that Böhm would have liked the building to be twice the size. Perhaps this is the reason why photographs are misleading: they tend to make the church look much bigger than it is.

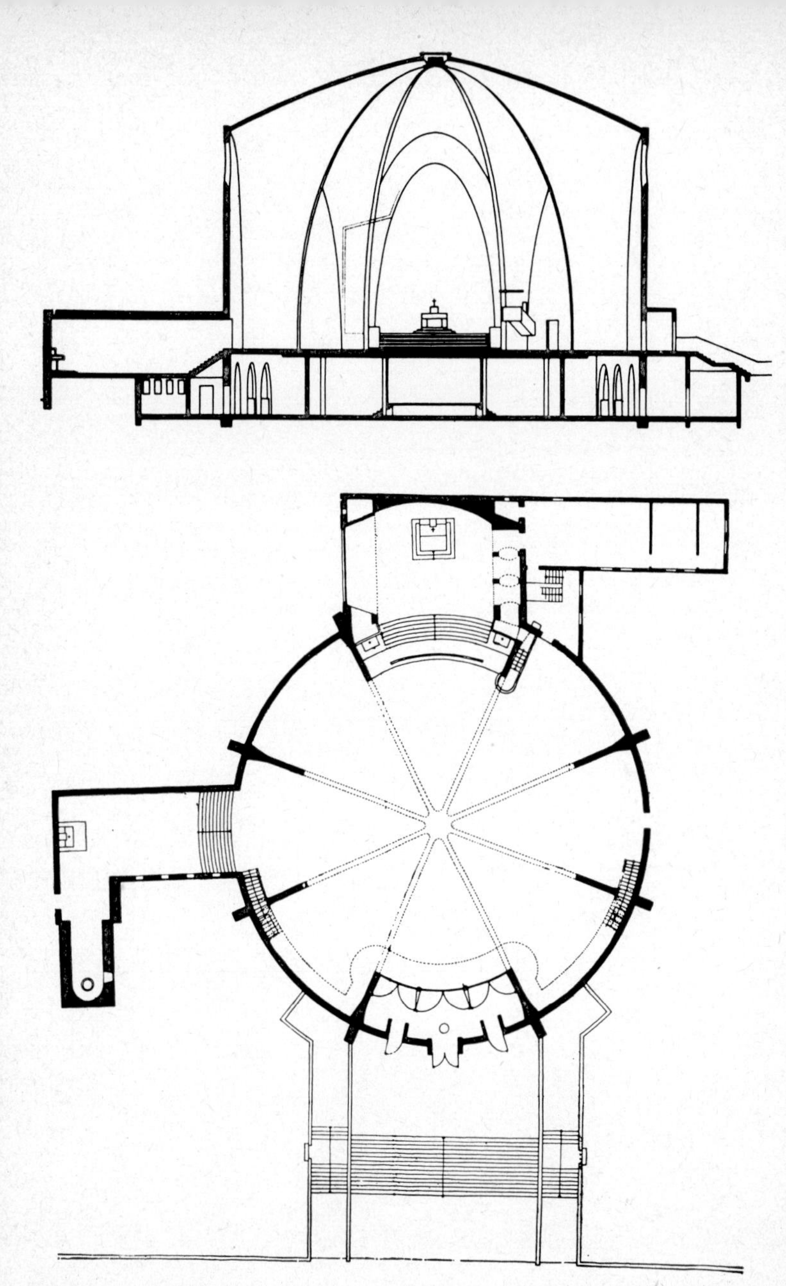

St Engelbert plan and section

St Engelbert

Rudolf Schwarz
ST ALBERT RC
LEVERSBACH · WEST GERMANY 1932–33

This is a small chapel, built by unemployed villagers during the slump at the request of a local teacher who was convinced that a church was needed if he was to continue his work.

In the words of Peter Hammond,[1] 'there are very few modern churches which will compare with it as an example of the possibilities of extreme simplicity, when simplicity is informed and illuminated by a sense of purpose. This is essentially a building to house an altar . . . a simple stone table, free-standing in the midst of an uncluttered sanctuary. It is impossible to describe the *style* of the building. It is no more "contemporary", in the popular sense of that word, than Gothic or Romanesque; it is simply an honest piece of construction. Yet this is one of the most completely satisfying buildings for worship that have been built in the last fifty years. Its poverty is not "insufficiency, frail weakness or pauperism". . . . Everything about this modest chapel is real; it rings true. Would that our own architects would study it, and learn from it that before building a church one must know what one is making.'

[1] Peter Hammond: *Liturgy and Architecture*, Barrie and Rockliff, London, 1960.

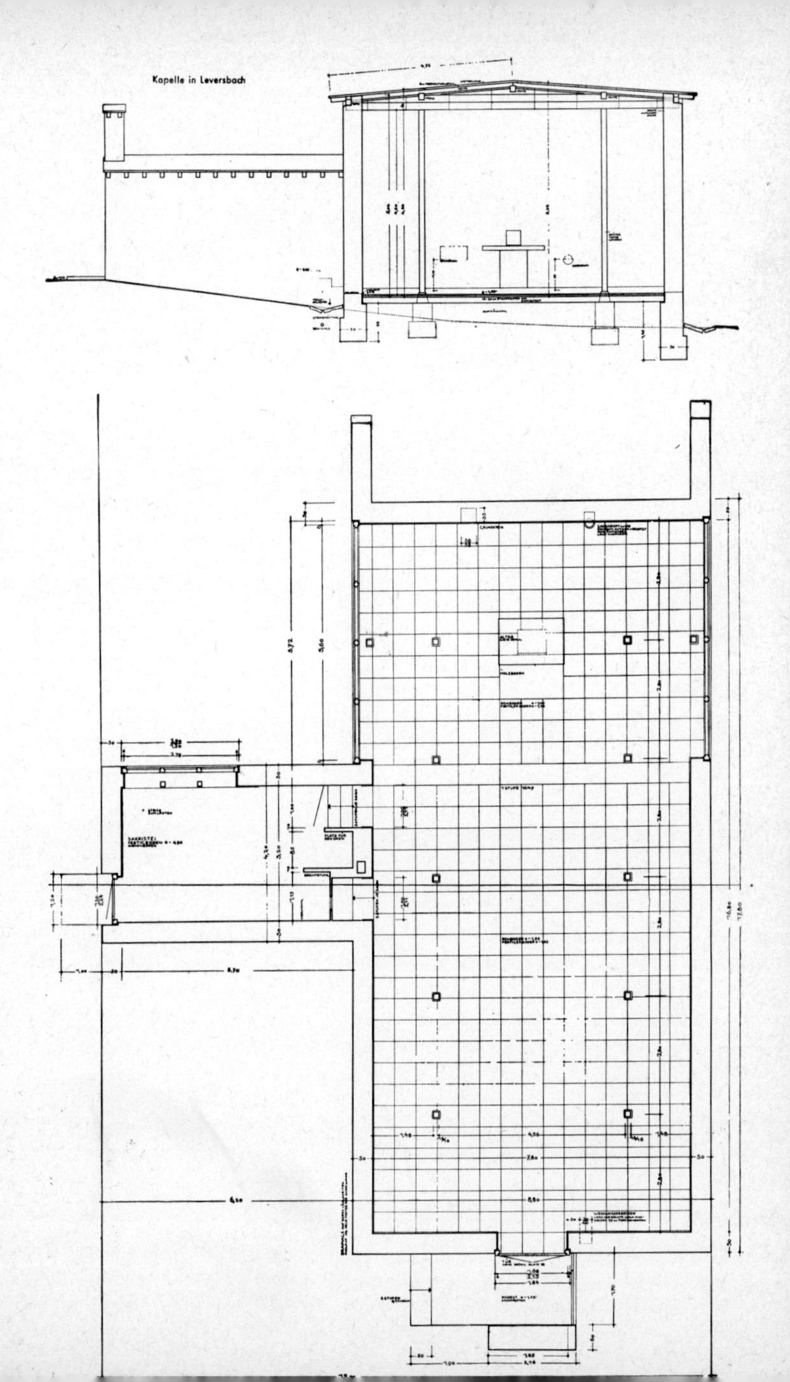

Kapelle in Leversbach

St Albert

Fritz Metzger
ST KARL RC
LUCERNE · SWITZERLAND 1935

After 1933 the Nazi régime increasingly prevented architectural experiment in Germany, and especially in church-building. Consequently the pioneer work was continued in Switzerland by those architects and churchmen who had had connections with the movement in Germany.

Fritz Metzger's church of St Karl is still one of the purest examples of a 'one-room' plan applied to a large church. The colonnade, outer wall and strip of windows over, flow round in a rhythmical semi-circular sweep uniting the spaces which would formerly have been called nave and sanctuary. The arrangement now seems as obvious as in its day it was revolutionary.

St Karl

St Karl

Werner M. Moser
CHURCH AT ZÜRICH-ALTSTETTEN Reformed
SWITZERLAND 1941

The blunt confrontation of the new church and social centre with the old village church at Altstetten is peculiarly Swiss. Careful grouping of the buildings and the usual Swiss attention to landscaping are the only *rapprochement*; otherwise, the old is old and the new is new, take it or leave it.

The idea of making an architectural statement about freedom from doctrinal rigidity by means of an asymmetrical composition of pulpit, communion table, font and cross along a 'broad front', is common in modern Protestant church-building. At the time when Moser designed the Altstetten church the idea was by no means new, but neither before nor since has it been carried out with such conviction and clarity. He has used the broad carved text to tie the composition together and to give it explicit meaning.

The attempt at a dynamic balance, reflecting the different character but interdependence of Baptism, the Eucharist, the Ministry of the Word and (counting the organ) of praise, is evident

in the work of all serious modern church architects. The asymmetrical 'broad front' composition has however a serious disadvantage: its relationship to the people remains rigid, the congregation are still onlookers or audience. Nor are its means truly architectural, but more like bas-relief; and the onlooking of the congregation can only be avoided by achieving a dynamic balance with the use of the full means of architecture—by making the distinctions between font, communion table and so on by organizing the whole space of the building in relation to them, so that there is no part of the space which is merely auditorium or seating-place, and the entire church is the holy place set apart for the people.

This church is remarkable also for the handling of its internal surfaces, many of which are synthetic, in the sense of being processed beyond the extent to which one could easily call them natural materials. Yet there is none of the tattiness which has become so closely associated with their use.

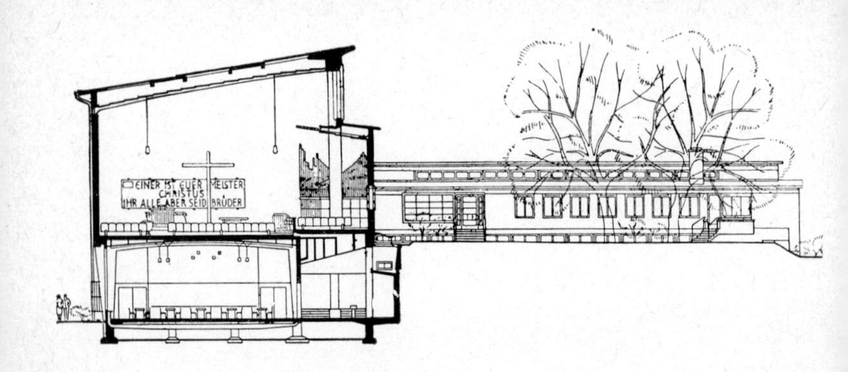

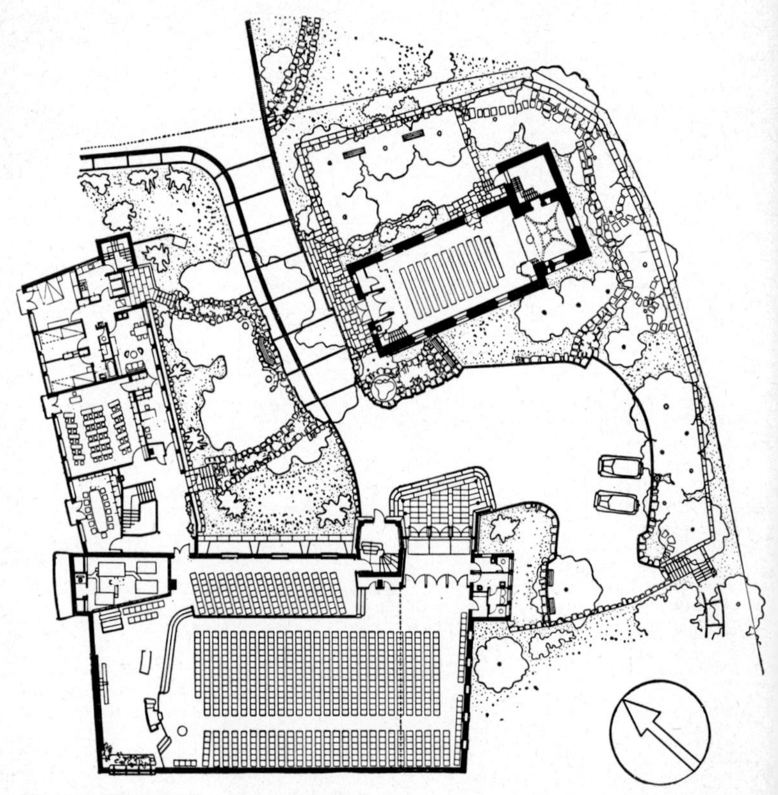

Church at Zürich-Alstetten plan and section

Church at Zürich-Altstetten

Le Corbusier
NOTRE-DAME DU HAUT RC
RONCHAMP · FRANCE 1952–55

What Le Corbusier has built and what he has written have profoundly affected architecture since 1920, so that a church by him would inevitably be important. What he has built at Ronchamp is something quite brilliant and original and unlike anything he or anybody else had built before.

Ronchamp is not a parish church but a pilgrimage chapel, and the site is on top of one of the highest hills in the district—an ancient, probably pre-Christian, holy place. Approaching Ronchamp from a distance, one sees the chapel white above the green waves of the Vosges hills; its strange shape is mysterious, exciting and attractive. It is not like a church and yet it is quite unlike any other kind of building. Outside it is complicated, without any obvious logic. It looks as if it might have grown in a night like a mushroom, and yet it could be very old; in spite of its complexity and apparent inconsistency, it is a unity and not a conglomeration of bits.

Inside it is like a grotto, or a set for a *fin-de-siècle* symbolist dance drama. The curved and sloping walls, the concave roof and the floor which slopes down towards the altar, are disorientating, creating a feeling of dreamlike unreality. This feeling is produced not only by the form of the building but by the scale, the materials and structure. The scale of the building is disturbing because it is incomprehensible; the structure is quite arbitrary. One wall of the church is twelve feet thick at its base, tapering to a foot at the top; superficially this looks solid but in fact it is made up of a reinforced concrete frame covered with chicken wire and sprayed with a thin skin of concrete which is whitened. It gives the feeling that it might be made of toothpaste. In the same way, the enormous concrete roof looks as if it might be inflated rubber, as it floats above the walls. The forms and materials are perverse, enhancing the dreamlike unreality of the whole. As a place for liturgy any barn would be better.

Le Corbusier seems to be trying to create the atmosphere of a primitive sacred place—to build a grotto. But as a grotto or sacred place Ronchamp is unconvincing; it is a folly, out of touch with any reality. This does not imply that Le Corbusier was insincere, or that the place is not a holy place, but that the building in spite of its brilliance does not seem to be the result of contact with any living reality.

Notre-Dame du Haut

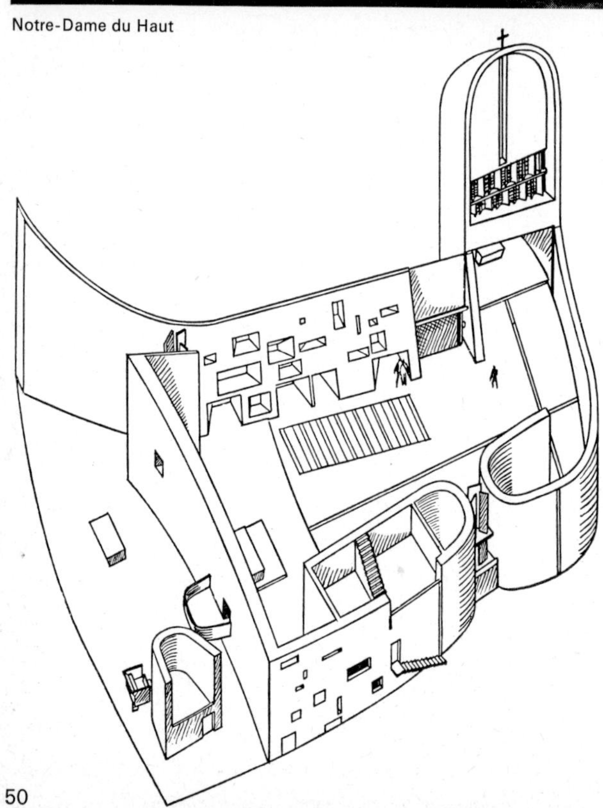

Particularly in church design, Ronchamp has provided a justification for architects to ignore any discipline, to pursue private whimsy without concern for function. Ronchamp does not diminish one's respect for Le Corbusier as an architect, because seen as a folly it is outstanding; but in the development of church building, it is a blind alley.

Notre-Dame du Haut

Le Corbusier
STE MARIE DE LA TOURETTE RC
EVEUX · FRANCE 1953–60

Le Corbusier built La Tourette on the insistence of Fr Couturier, who was one of the originators of the policy which has been called *Appel aux maîtres au dehors*. This policy encouraged Churches to commission artists and architects who were not practising Christians, because the integrity of their work contrasted strongly with bogus, pseudo-religious church art and architecture.

La Tourette is a Dominican house of studies designed to accommodate both teaching and the needs of the spiritual life. It is closely organized and tightly packed into a small space; this has resulted in an elaborate and romantic complex of buildings. By contrast the main church is a radically plain building, a concrete cuboid with a strange kidney-shaped chapel of the Blessed Sacrament attached to it on one side. At a lower level, out of sight of the main church but spatially related to it, are altars for private masses. The church is on the highest part of the site so that you go into it from below. As at the Dominican Priory at Lille, the choir is at one end, next to it the altar, then more seating.

Le Corbusier has written that he builds 'in light, with light'. The main church is rather dark; at the choir end there are low windows lighting the stalls, and a strip of light high up lighting the underside of the roof, which is pierced with a square flue in the centre above the choir. The other end of the church is lit through a vertical slit. The brightest place is the Blessed Sacrament chapel, lit from above by circular flues letting in light and containing light. The concrete of the church is rough almost to ugliness; but for the proportions and the light, this church could be a fearful prison. The building is stripped down, hard, poor, yet light and radiant; it is silent and empty with the silence and emptiness of the tomb, but transfigured by light.

Le Corbusier has always been sensitive to the life of the people for whom he builds. Here, in contrast to his chapel at Ronchamp (p. 48) he has been able, without being personally involved in the life, to make a building in which it can flourish.

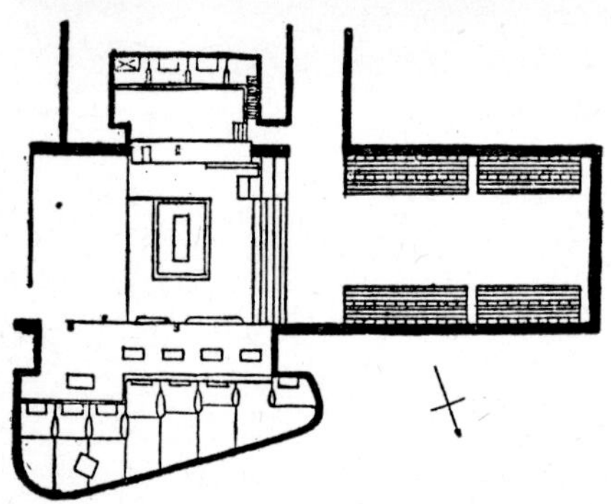

Ste Marie de la Tourette

Dominikus Böhm
ST MARIA-KÖNIGIN RC
MARIENBURG, COLOGNE · WEST GERMANY 1954

This is the last church built by Dominikus Böhm, who died in 1955. It is on the other side of Cologne from Rudolf Schwarz's last church, St Christophorus: they have a lot in common.

Böhm's long and productive life spans the periods of Historical Revivalism, Art Nouveau, International Style, and the post-war period of modern architecture. The monograph published in 1962 by Verlag Schnell and Steiner, Munich, shows the great variety and originality of his work.

St Maria-Königin has a lovely site among pine trees, where the church sits gently. This unassuming quietness is in sympathy with the movement in Germany (and to some extent elsewhere) away from grand churches and towards smaller buildings and congregations, in which each person can be related to the other and to the action of the liturgy. In this context the comparison with St Engelbert at Cologne built by Böhm in 1932 (p. 34) is fas-

cinating because of the difference in size and the different attitude to scale in the two buildings.

There are four columns standing in the space of the church. This four-column structure has been used in several of the best new churches; all are buildings where the places of the altar and the people have been closely related. At St Maria-Königin, in spite of the stained glass wall through which one would expect the space to leak, the columns have succeeded in creating a 'place'.

Beside the main church and leading down from it, there is an attached circular baptistery. Like the church, the stained glass—designed by Böhm himself—is cool and unostentatious.

The building is a wonderful conclusion to Böhm's work, in which he was able both to lead and remain in touch with the development of the mind of the Church.

St Maria-Königin

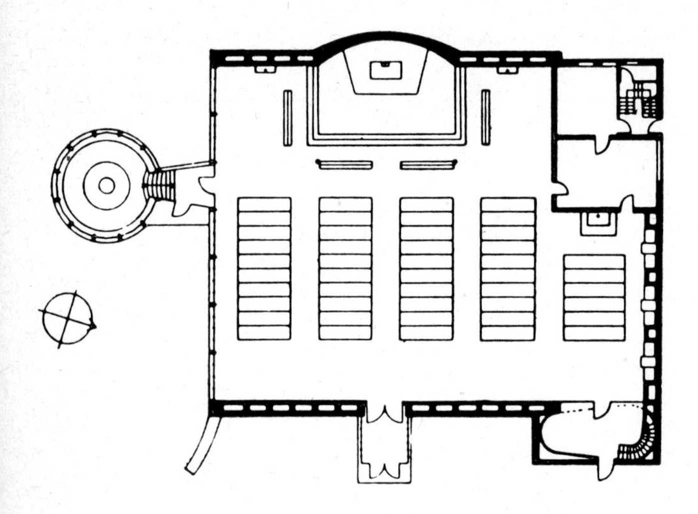

St Maria-Königin plan

St Maria-Königin

Pinsard and Hutchinson
DOMINICAN PRIORY CHURCH RC
LILLE · FRANCE 1954–58

Monks have played an important part in originating the Liturgical Movement and the revival of church architecture which has developed with it. Although they have often been the most reactionary elements in the life of the Church, the absolute commitment of monastic life can be the setting for very radical thinking.

At Lille, the Dominican Priory Church is a basic building like a factory. The elements from which it is made can be directly appreciated; the unplastered concrete vault is supported by columns, which rise directly from the floor close to (but in front of) the face of the clerestory wall, which runs uninterrupted from end to end of the church. At the top, the walls are stiffened with a hori-

zontal membrane through which the columns pass. The clerestory walls sit on the aisle roofs, which are supported by a thickening of the columns. Under the roof the main windows run in the plane of the walls past the columns. This mannerist, somewhat elaborate way in which elements are both distinguished and combined, has a structural vitality which works. Two elements in this system do not quite come off—the bulge of the columns which supports the aisle roofs, and the holes in the clerestory wall. The bulge lacks the elementary clarity of the rest, the glazed holes seem fussy.

Lille is an industrial area. The church is built from materials which relate it to the local industrial vernacular and so relate the church and priory to the life around it; whereas, in the nineteenth century, the Gothic revival church dissociated itself from the contemporary environment.

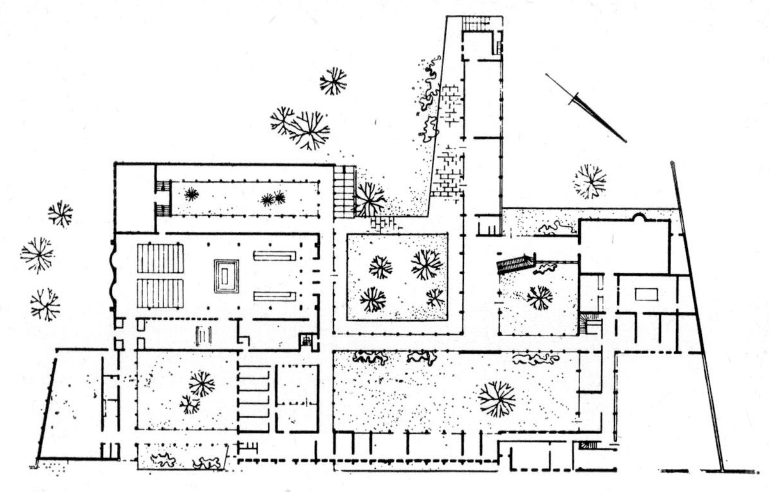

Dominican Priory Church plan

André Le Donné
CHURCH AT MARIENAU-LES-FORBACH RC
FRANCE 1955

This is a small country church with a simple economical structure. In its liturgical organization it shows that the architect and the community which he is building for are really in touch with the liturgical reawakening. The kind of space, the position of the tabernacle and reading and preaching places, font, etc., all confirm this. Without great pretensions it fulfils the needs of a local community; it works as a church. Probably few modern Roman Catholic churches work better, though they may be more exciting and better architecture.

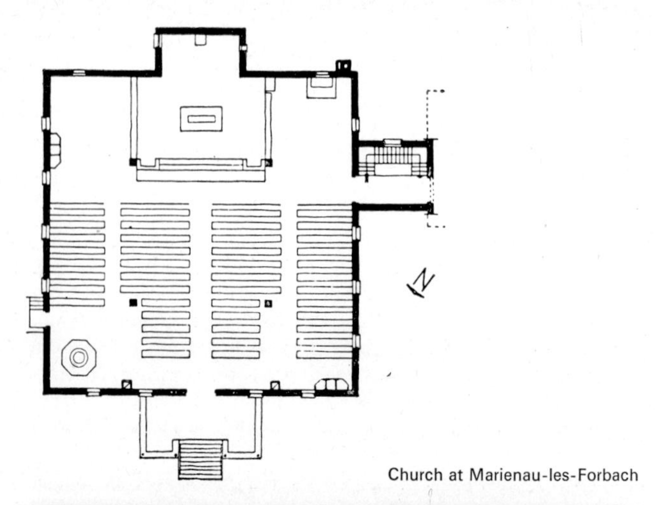

Church at Marienau-les-Forbach

In Orthodox countries on the Mediterranean, innumerable village communities have been admirably served by the simplest kind of church which is no more than a barn with an apse. This church by Le Donné is not quite so simple, but it is the kind of simple idea for a church which could be developed in many ways to fulfil the need, in town as well as country, for good, unpretentious small churches.

Church at Marienau-les-Forbach

Gottfried Böhm
ST ALBERT RC
SAARBRÜCKEN · WEST GERMANY 1955

Usually liked or disliked strongly for its use of an elaborate reinforced concrete structural system, this church is seldom recognized as a very advanced liturgical experiment. This may be due partly to the furnishings, which have been put in since the photographs we show here were taken: among them are a very large organ and rigid seating, both of which tend to destroy the quality of the internal space—a quality which depends on the consistent and simple handling of a complex spatial idea. The idea itself goes back to (perhaps before) a project by Dominikus Böhm of 1923, which, one may conjecture, never came to fruition because at that time neither the liturgical readiness nor the structural know-how existed for its development. It depends upon the definition of the whole church space by an enclosing wall—the clear setting-apart of a 'place'—and the intensification of this 'placeness' at the main centre of liturgical action, the altar, by means of columns which enclose without dividing, which set apart yet allow access. To relate these two places so that the second is still part of the first, and without putting the altar inappropriately at dead-centre (a temptation to which architects can and do easily succumb) requires considerable spatial and structural skill, and in this church the younger Böhm comes near to bringing his father's intuitive scheme to maturity.

The main weakness of the interior is that all the surfaces (except

the columns) are suspended from the wholly external main structure, so that from inside there is no way of seeing how they arrive there. There is no manifestly 'built' feeling about them; they appear thin and unreal.

Something similar is true of the altar: the support is carved from one great block of stone, yet the rubberiness of the sculptural form—for all its expressionism around the *idea* of supporting on finger-tips—denies the fact of having been built, set up. This is in contrast to its setting within the architectural space, for the columns, communion step and the three steps making a 'holy hill' have an inevitability about them which is extremely rare.

The font is in a small baptistery under the tower, separated from the church by an entrance porch. The steps down, the circular well of a room, and the form of the font combine to give a thoroughly convincing context for water; and the water itself is alive, bubbling up into the font and gushing out—a straightforward baptismal symbolism which no amount of extraneous art could ever equal.

The organization of separate small baptistery, entrance, altar and chapel of reservation (in that order) along an axis, shows the architect's concern for the meaningfulness of the aspects of the Christian life to which these things relate. The scheme is however static and rather cerebral compared with the dynamic quality of the main church space, and reflects an earlier attitude to liturgical worship.

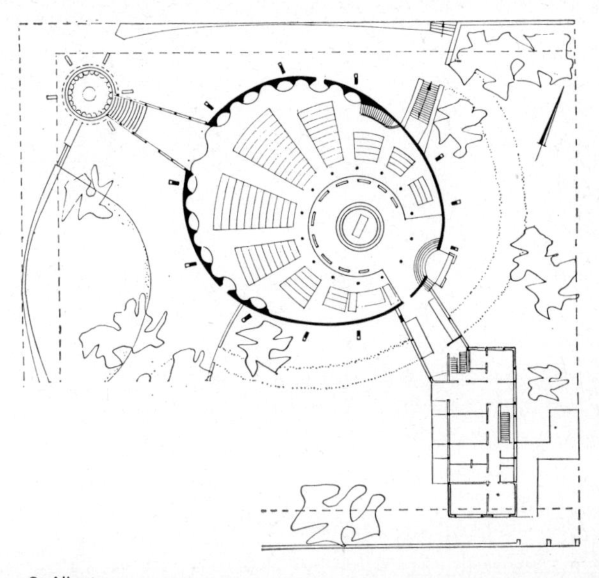
St Albert

Kaija and Heikki Siren
CHAPEL AT OTANIEMI Lutheran
NEAR HELSINKI · FINLAND 1956

The chapel, part of a Technical University which has been planned by Alvar Aalto, is a very beautiful example of a preoccupation of architects throughout the world with the relating of simple, sympathetic materials. The floor and walls are of local red brick, the roof structure and ceiling are timber, the roof-covering asbestos cement. Great care has been taken with the relationships and junctions between these materials. This modern preoccupation with materials descends from the British Arts and Crafts Movement with its love of vernacular architecture, and from the international interest in Japanese traditions of building.

The use of the materials and the 'economy' of the building give the impression of a functional motivation. But though this is a Lutheran church, its primary formative function doesn't seem to be the liturgy. The glass wall opening on to the forest behind the sanctuary, and the reduction of the sanctuary furnishings, could not have been the consequence of such a concern; the function for which the chapel seems to be designed is silent prayer and withdrawal. This has a definite place in the Christian life as shown in the New Testament. ('In the morning a great while before day, he rose and went out to a lonely place, and there he prayed'.) But such an order of priorities is unusual; churches have more often been built for the liturgy or for preaching. Churches and particularly chapels in the wilderness, however, have been used in this way. A place with a view for prayer is not an innovation. It is in the monastic tradition of the Eastern Churches; on Mount Athos, for instance, the hermitage or monk's cell is orientated with a view

Chapel at Otaniemi

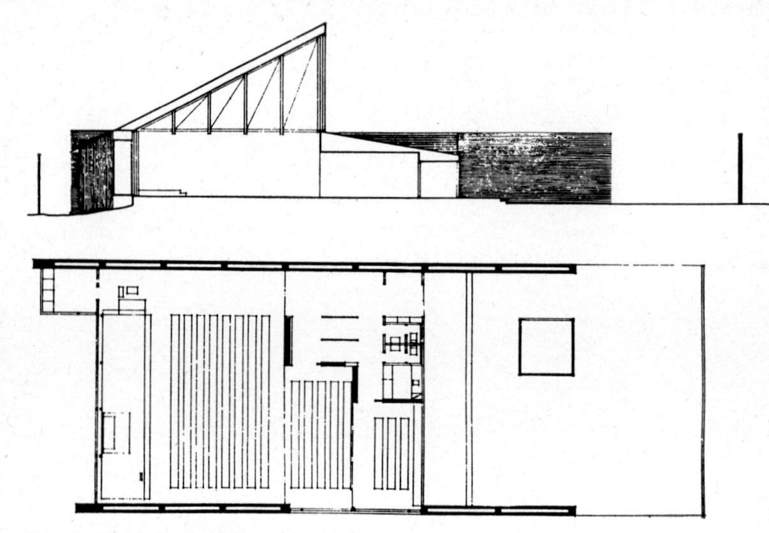

Chapel at Otaniemi plan and section

of the horizon between sea and sky, or of a mountain or rock. And in the far east the choice of monastic sites has been governed by similar considerations. The feeling of this chapel is closer to that of a Zen monastic garden, an Athonite cell or a Benedictine cloister than to that of most churches.

Chapel at Otaniemi

Arbeitsgruppe 4 (W. Holzbauer, F. Kurrent, J. Spalt)
HEILIGEN BLUT RC
SALZBURG-PARSCH · AUSTRIA 1956

It is often said of an old barn that it would make a good church. Many farm buildings have a down-to-earth 'rightness' about them, a lack of pretension, which is also one of the qualities of a good church. But when converted—as many have been—they usually lose that quality in the process. The temptation for the architect to do something clever is too great.

This church, in a suburb of Salzburg, is an exception. It is converted from an old manor farm, of the kind that has house, barn and stable under one roof. The stable had an ancient vault supported on slender granite columns, and this has been retained, along with the outside walls. Beyond the low vault, the height extends into the roof-space of the old building, and in this light-filled place the altar is set up, on free-standing steps—a symbolic holy hill in contrast to the great black sheet of floor. Because of this powerful floor, the taut continuity of the enclosing (pure white) walls, and the lowering of the space on the opposite side of the altar, with more seats and two more columns, the whole interior remains one unified space. This is remarkable considering the contrasts in height; the architects have not only a great (and rare) feeling for the symbolic functions of a church, but also the true architectural skill to give them appropriate form.

The pulpit is related to the space of the church through its position on the enclosing wall; in this way it is distinguished in function from the altar. The font stands to one side under the high space, a little indeterminate in position.

The upper roof has been extended to give protection against glare to the great skylight, and the space underneath has been used to house the bells. The upper storey above the vault has been used as a hall, again extended into the roof-space to keep the walls low. The external scale produced by the juxtaposition of these two arrangements is entirely satisfying.

Heiligen Blut

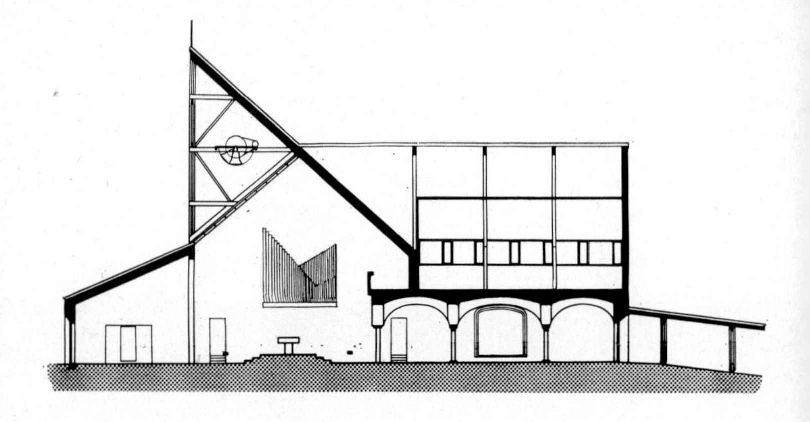

Heiligen Blut plan and section

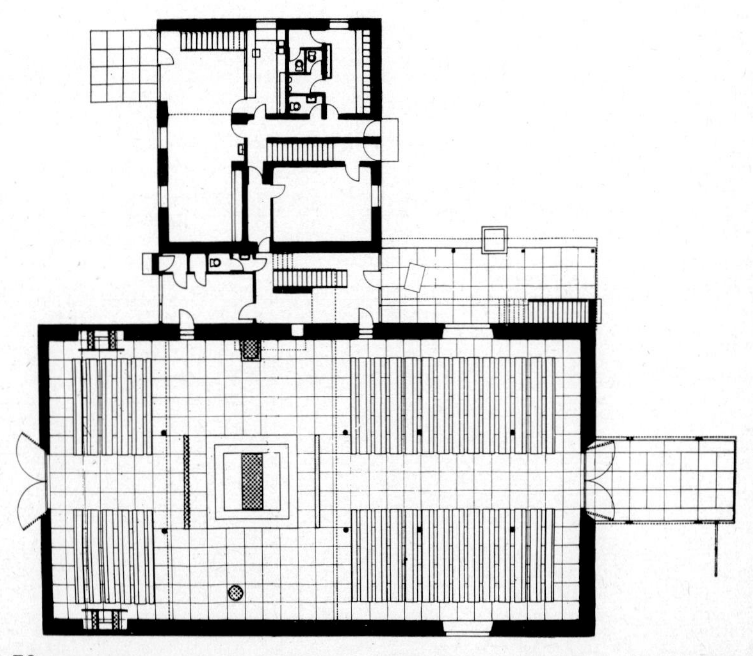

Emil Steffann and Siegfried Ostreicher
ST LAURENTIUS RC
GERN, MUNICH · WEST GERMANY 1956

Emil Steffann has built a number of churches in a thick-walled, arched, chunky brick style reminiscent of Romanesque, but down-to-earth in the manner of old farm buildings. Traditional elements such as apses and aisles are used for what they *do*, and only in situations where what they do is appropriate to what is needed. St Laurentius at Gern is the best example of this refreshing approach, which restores the true meaning of tradition and can produce buildings that achieve all that more superficially 'modern' buildings intend.

The large apse is placed on the *side* of the building, making a 'place' half-way down its length, so that the directional drive of the great pitched roof is cancelled out, or rather made to work from both directions inward to the centre. What would have formerly been called an aisle therefore becomes a narthex, a space related to, yet slightly withdrawn from, the main space of the church—a gentle transition from the world outside to the set-apart place within.

The design of the sanctuary is remarkable; it is one of the very few examples of a complete integration of all the essential elements with one another and with the space of the church. The idea has connections with the *bema* of some Early Christian churches, and relies on a resolved tension between the altar and the seat for the celebrant and his assistants, the step of which is the preaching-place. The communion rail, which can so easily form a barrier between the congregation and the liturgical action, avoids this by being very light in contrast to the solidity of the other, essentially 'built', set-up elements. The altar itself is unpretentious, its character relying on the rightness of its form in relation to the material of which it is made. Compare the altar of St Albert, Saarbrücken (p. 66), which is also of stone, but whose forms are those of a stone reclining figure rather than of a stone altar; both stoniness and altarness are lost.

Mainly because its forms are unfashionable, St Laurentius has been largely overlooked and its significance underrated. It is, however, the product of a developed understanding of liturgical relationships and distinctions, on the part of both the architects and the Church in Munich. First-rate churches can only come as the result of such a shared understanding between architect and client.

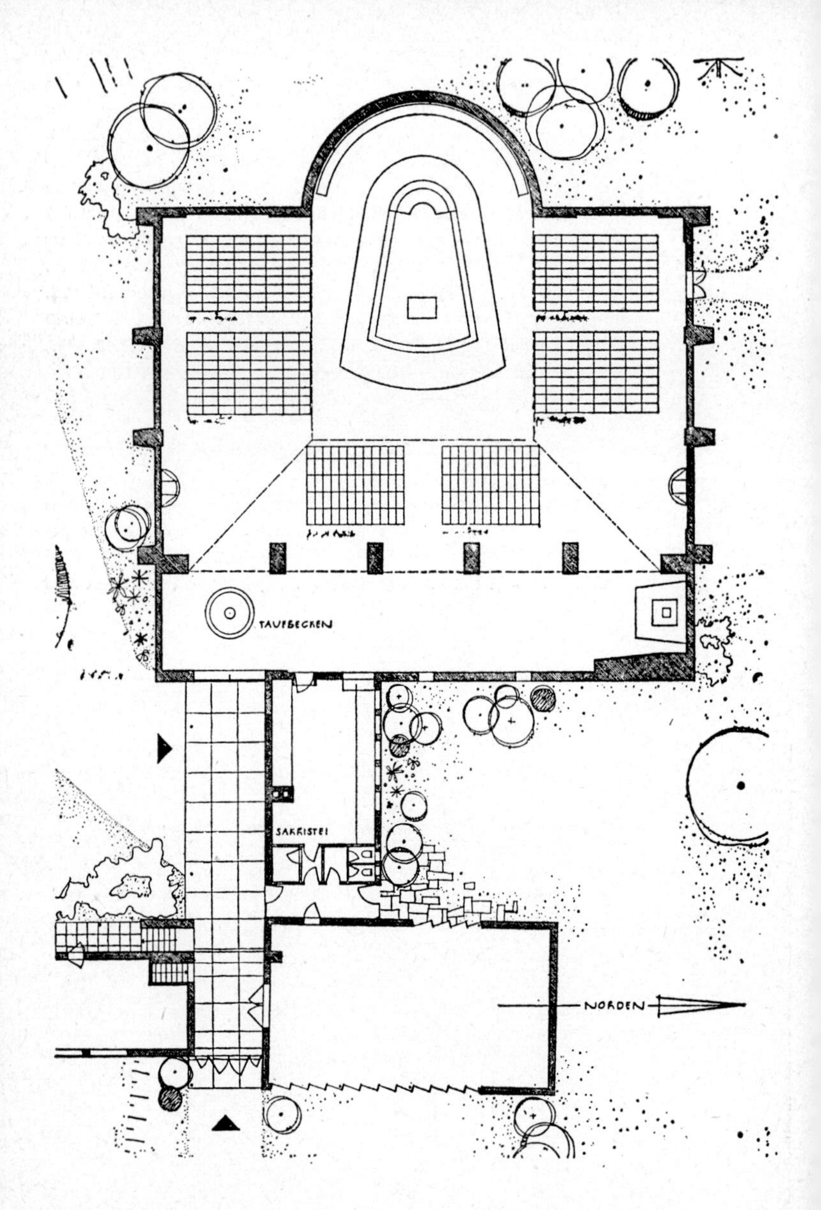

St Laurentius plan

St Laurentius

St Laurentius

Rudolf Schwarz
ST ANNA RC
DÜREN · WEST GERMANY 1956

Stones from the old church of St Anna, which had been a place of pilgrimage and was destroyed in the war, were used for this new church. The theme of reconstruction out of the ashes, with new walls from the old heap, was a source of inspiration to Schwarz, as indeed it was to others after the war. Schwarz, however, was never caught in the net of sentimentality which surrounded many such enterprises (as we feel was the case, for example, with the treatment of the ruins of the old Coventry Cathedral). He saw the stones in their old clear symbolic nature, as possessing strength and permanence when built together into a wall, just as the Apostle Peter described the Christian people.

The walls of St Anna's rise solid and sheer. The one departure which Schwarz has permitted himself is the 'tree' of stones and jewel-like glass lenses behind the altar as viewed from the longer of the two naves, the assembly-place of the larger congregations of pilgrims. This is a complex piece of expressionism, and is not overplayed; its forms are still in the nature of masonry, and while it represents the Tree of Life, with its connection with the Resurrection, it is also expressive of the stones themselves rising again out of the chaos of destruction.

The shorter nave, at right angles to the larger, is more specifically the parish church and, for liturgical worship on the more normal scale of the parish, is the more satisfactory. In the space between the two arms of the **L** of the naves is a low, wide, darker space through which one enters. Here, near the door, is the font—a beautifully apt container for water, like a hollowed-out water-worn boulder—and further along is a small altar, reliquary and votive lights. This low 'aisle' is empty of seats, and its strong horizontality links the two naves and prevents the building being split into two separate churches; as also does the powerful presence of the great square of the main altar, which relates to both naves.

The kind of space which Schwarz has created in St Anna's has great affinities with his early church of Corpus Christi at Aachen (p. 22). The wide, low side-aisle, used as an entrance-space and baptistery, from which the main space of the church unfolds gently, is a recurrent theme in Schwarz's churches, although he never became 'stuck' with it: he made it work better as he developed it, and St Anna's is a beautiful example of its subtlety in skilful hands.

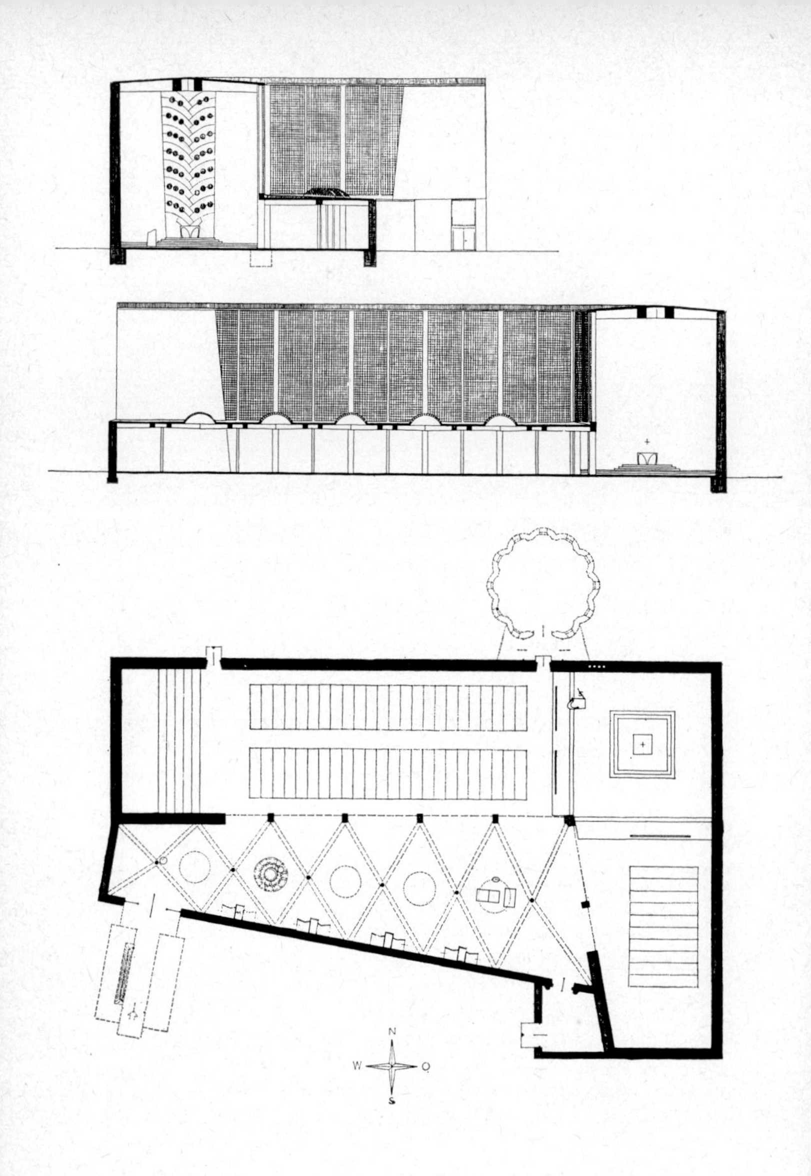

St Anna plan and section

St Anna

Rudolf Schwarz
HEILIGE FAMILIE RC
OBERHAUSEN · WEST GERMANY 1956–58

This is an experiment with a dead-square plan and a central sanctuary. The symbolic attractions of such a layout are obvious, the liturgical disadvantages great. Schwarz has achieved a satisfactory but precarious balance by virtue of placing the altar off-centre in the sanctuary, leaving a full quarter of the church unseated (though at the side where clear space is least useful) and by the use of a four-column structure which places the sanctuary firmly in the space of the building and avoids a lop-sided feeling.

This is the first of a series of projects and completed churches which seem to show a new inspiration towards the end of Schwarz's life; his liturgical understanding and his architectural skill and feeling come together more closely in a quickening of creativeness. He evidently felt the central sanctuary to be inappropriate, despite his clever handling of the problems it presented, and eventually developed an entirely resolved version without it in St Christophorus at Niehl, Cologne (p. 116).

The ground-level enclosing wall at Oberhausen continues beyond the church around an atrium, part of which is roofed to form a combined baptistery and week-day chapel. The transition from the busy world outside to the firmly set-apart place of the church is gradual—a return to an ancient principle which seems particularly apt to the church in the modern city.

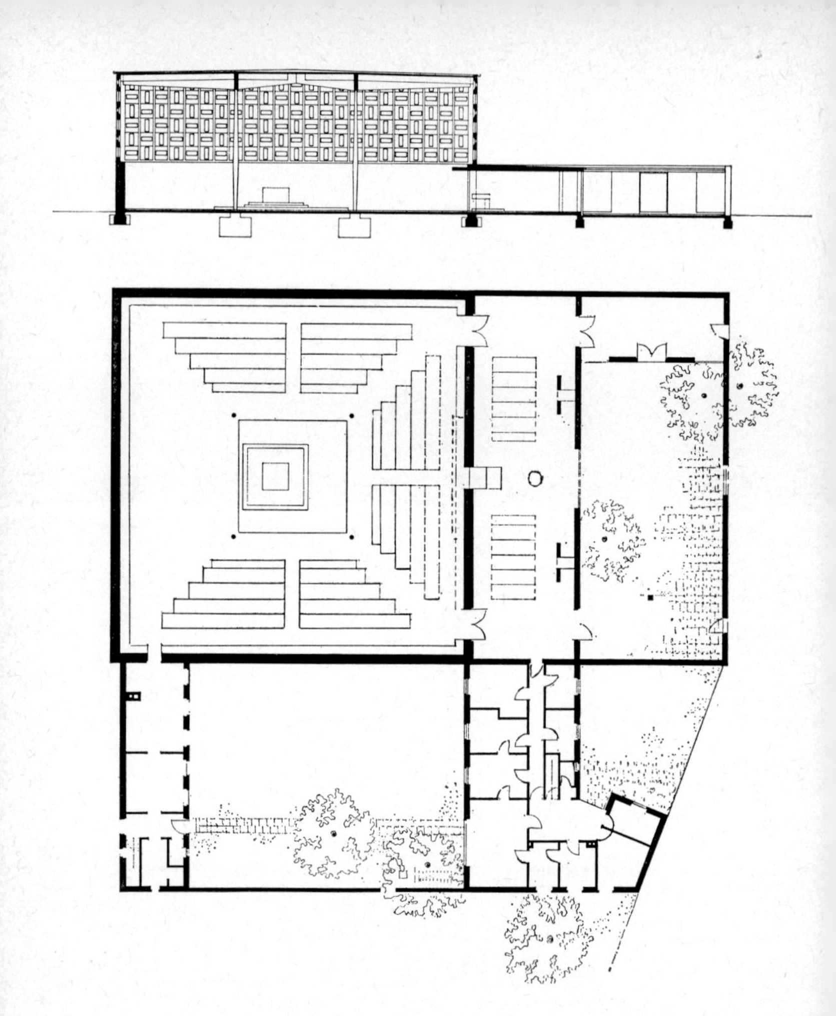

Heilige Familie plan and section

Heilige Familie

Heilige Familie

Robert Maguire and Keith Murray
ST PAUL Anglican
BOW COMMON, LONDON · ENGLAND 1956–60

'A church is a place for the assembly of the people of God. It is a holy place, consecrated, set apart for this purpose.' While these two linked ideas were the basis of the design, it was developed to fulfil the special needs of the place and a particular Christian community. For instance, while the church had to be able to seat 500 people its normal congregation would be much smaller. The central space within the colonnade and the continuous aisles around it are so arranged that a small congregation within the columns will not feel lost, since the columns, white and brightly lit on their inner faces, produce a strong feeling of enclosure. On the other hand, these columns do not cut off people in the lower aisles, since the form of the aisle roofs projects the space towards the centre.

The church may be seen as a pattern of relationships, which are significant because of their function in the context of an actual liturgy; a liturgy seen as a movement towards the place of the altar and communion, a movement towards the light. In this church the movement is inwards through the dark porch, past the font, through the procession to the place of the Ministry of the Word—synaxis—into the light of the sanctuary. In this the colonnade, and hanging corona of lights around the sanctuary, and the ciborium define the spaces without preventing free movement between them.

St Paul

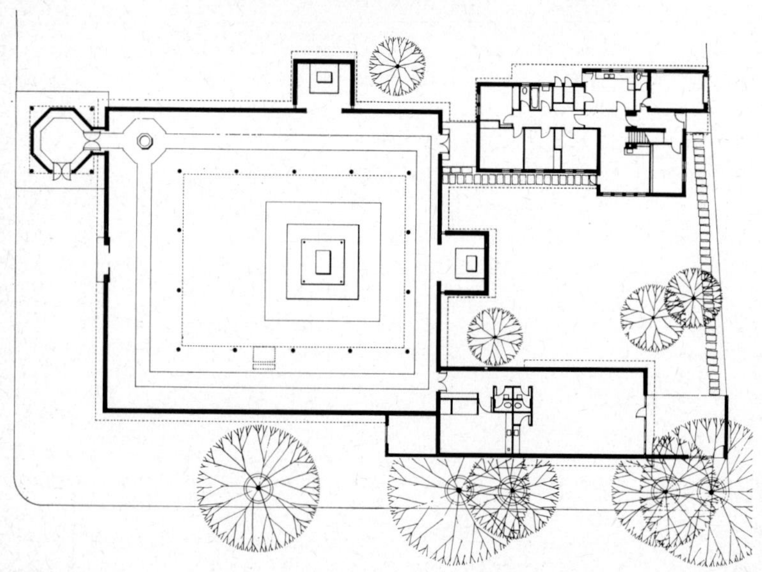

St Paul plan

The church is built out of cheap flint brick and fair-faced concrete, exposed rolled steel sections and ordinary concrete paving slabs like the pavement of the street outside; each thing carefully done, an affirmation of the intrinsic value of ordinary industrial materials and good work. Contrasted with these materials will be mosaics of angels in the panels above the columns.

St Paul

Joachim Schürmann
ST PIUS X RC
FLITTARD, COLOGNE · WEST GERMANY 1957–60

The apparent simplicity of this church is deceptive; it is the result of the ease and grace with which a quite complex spatial and structural idea has been made to work. Structure and space are so nearly integrated that there is little feeling that the structure has been put in to hold up a set of surfaces dictated by the spatial organization of the building, or that the structure has dictated the organization of the space. Nor, further, does one feel that these two in their happy relationship have become an autonomous expression of the architect's manipulative skill, for together they serve the building's purpose very closely.

This is not to say that there is no shoe-horning of functions into the building. The position, for example, of the font is arbitrary, and one is tempted to the conclusion that in the end this was simply a nice-looking place to put it. The confessionals, too, have grown very large and important, their podiums suggesting liturgical solemnity, and one suspects that some filling-out of the side-aisle was thought necessary. But for all that, the interior is unmistakably that of a church; it could not be that of any other kind of building—a statement that can be made of few modern churches. The essential church character is moreover achieved by wholly architectural means; by the integration of space and structure already mentioned, by the considered use of light, without a single trick or recourse to the methods of stage-lighting (again, rare among modern churches), and by eschewing even the last vestiges of historical association.

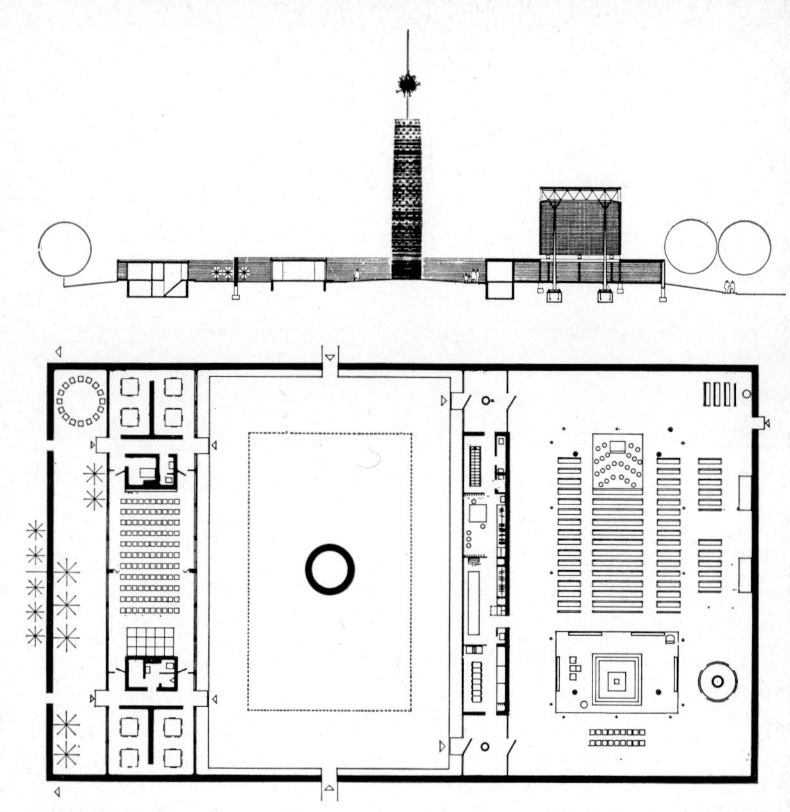

St Pius X plan and section

St Pius X

The brick wall at ground level delineates the extent of the whole church precinct, enclosing church, atrium and parish centre. The plain ceiling of the continuous aisle or ambulatory strengthens the enclosure, making it firm and positive but in an ordinary familar way: it is completely unaffected, the kind of enclosure we know and understand—basic architecture.

The central space breaks through this, pushing upwards into light, its four tapered white columns spreading into the roof structure from which hangs the thin scaly curtain of clerestory wall. The space is a little like that under a weeping willow tree, with support, roof and wall in one continuous structure filled with light; or it would be, were the hanging quality of the clerestory wall not almost completely negated by the spindly columns immediately beneath it. The lower strip of window does not in itself proclaim that what is below it is propped up, while that above it hangs down; and the thinness of the outer columns takes away the strength of the lower ceiling at the very point where it needs strength most. There seems to be a loss of nerve here.

The four large columns, standing in the light-filled space, complete what the outer wall begins, transforming the church from a mere interior to a 'place', a holy place, set apart, the place of the Christian people. And this place has no one-way direction, even though the sanctuary is at one end with the seating facing it. The quality of placeness is what gives rise to the apparent simplicity: an expression of the unity of the Church, but achieved through a complexity which reflects the varying relationships between the hierarchic levels of the Church in the Church's worship, and allows flexibility in those relationships.

Angelo Mangiarotti and Bruno Morassuti
CHURCH AT BARANZATE RC
MILAN · ITALY 1957

Seen from a distance this church stands out, clean and bright, if a little unreal, with the *panache* of Italian industrial design; but as it hasn't worn too well it is rather disappointing closer to. Unlike the outside, the inside is relatively unphotogenic, because it is difficult to appreciate the quality of space in a photograph. It is beautiful and light, even on a rainy day. On coming up from the baptistery in the plinth, one can immediately appreciate the whole church; it is simple, clear and comprehensible. Four magnificent columns support the roof; the space is enclosed by translucent walls. The space is like that in a great marquee or a grove of trees. The columns, like tent poles or tree trunks, create a space around them which is contained by the membrane of the wall.

The remarkable unity of the space mitigates the weakness of the planning of the interior, which gives the impression of a modern building re-ordered for a medieval liturgy. Surprisingly there is a feeling of a church divided into chancel and nave. This seems to result from a number of quite small things working together. The most important of them is the near-alignment of the front step of the sanctuary, the crucifix and the sanctuary lamp, with one pair of the columns; all these create a plane between the altar and the seating place, a plane with some of the significance of a chancel arch.

There is a crypt on the same level as the baptistery. The chapel in the crypt is a dark complement to the light church. Hidden in the earth of the plinth, it is cool in summer; a place for private prayer and recollection, dedicated to the Mother of God.

Church at Baranzate

Church at Baranzate

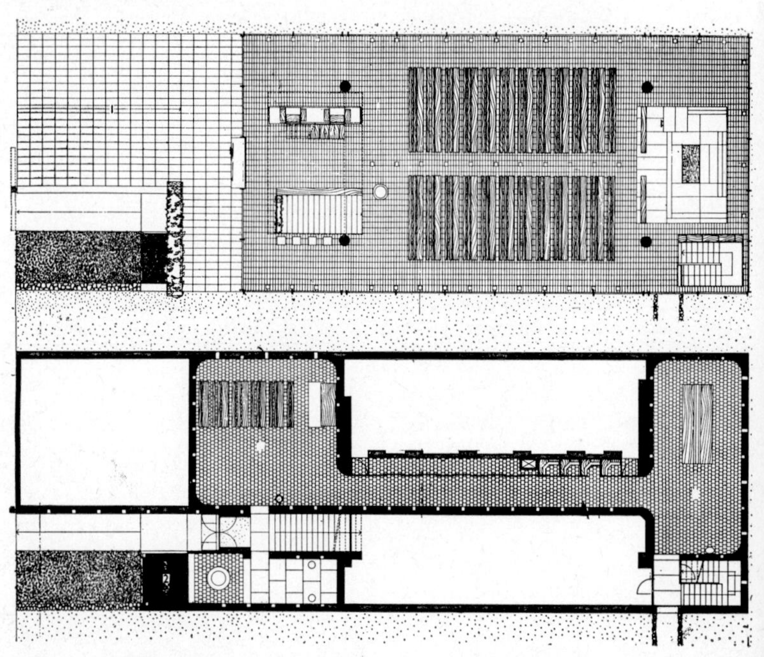

Church at Baranzate plans

MATRI MISERICORDIAE

St André

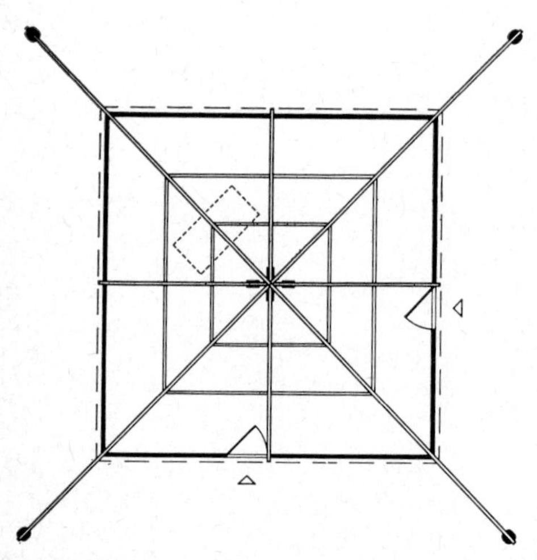
St André plan

Rainer Senn
ST ANDRÉ RC
NICE · FRANCE 1957

A recurrent preoccupation among modern theologians of all denominations is a return to simplicity: on one level the stripping away of ritual accretions which obscure the meaning of liturgical worship, on another the expression of a Christian simplicity of life; and in the field of church-building the renunciation of all pretension and artiness and a return to straightforward, down-to-earth building.

No other modern church is so down-to-earth as Rainer Senn's little chapel for the Abbé Pierre's community of rag-sorters. Peter Hammond has described it[1] as 'an outward embodiment of a community which has nothing and which yet possesses all things, a true image of the temple built of living stones'. It was built by the architect himself and a friend at a total cost of fifty pounds, using a scaffold of old bed-springs. Its walls are of unsquared off-cuts of logs and its floor of loose pebbles.

[1] Peter Hammond: *Liturgy and Architecture*, Barrie and Rockliff, London, 1960.

St André

Alvar Aalto
VUOKSENNISKA CHURCH Lutheran
IMATRA · FINLAND 1958

This is an extraordinary building by one of the great masters of modern architecture, a *tour de force* which commands respect, whatever doubts one may have about its relevance to the liturgical issues now confronting church architects. Reyner Banham has written[1] of an 'unobvious, devious, obtuse and almost grudging charm that gives nothing away at first sight . . . but yields more and more to whoever is prepared to work away at it'.

Inside, it is a vast space whose complicated organization hinges around its division into three separate rooms for various parish activities. The method by which the division is accomplished—two large sliding screens which roll away on curved tracks into slots in the walls—gives rise to a series of brilliantly handled architectural surprises which largely determine the character of the space. But as a church, it makes no contribution to the debate which is exercising theologians and architects throughout the west: it remains a great auditorium.

[1] Reyner Banham: *Guide to Modern Architecture*, Architectural Press, London, 1962.

Vuoksenniska Church

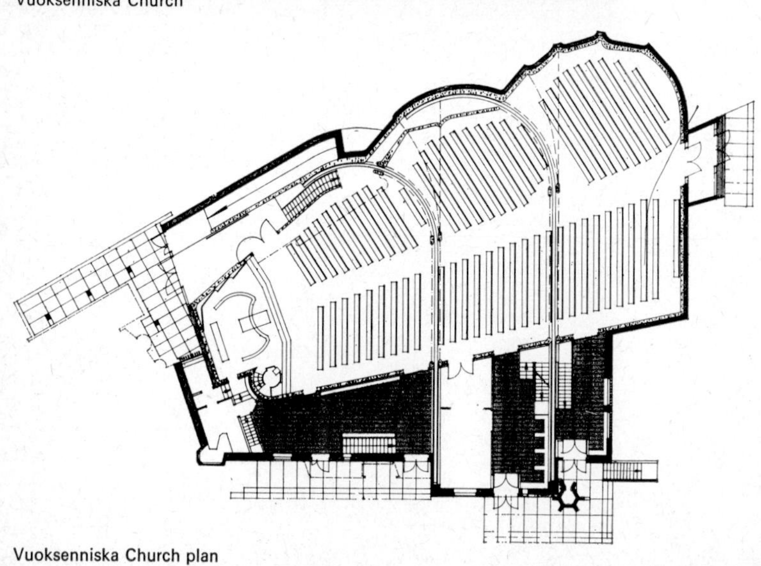

Vuoksenniska Church plan

Holger Jensen (in association with Edward Armstrong and Frederick MacManus)
DANISH SEAMEN'S CHURCH Lutheran
STEPNEY, LONDON · ENGLAND 1959

This church has a difficult little site, dominated by two roads and a railway. As well as the church, there are rooms where the crews of Danish ships can go when they are on shore in London. The main way into the building has been very carefully handled. The path passes under a pergola of white beams to the doors; the space of the passage narrows around the corner of the church, the brick wall wrapping round the church and jutting into the entrance way. The strong corner makes one aware of the strength of the cube of the church within the complex of building.

On plan the church is only twenty-five feet by twenty-seven feet, seating sixty-five people. It is really only a large room, and yet its quality as a space gives it an authority lacking in most modern churches, large or small. A few good architectural elements have been chosen, related precisely and carried out in two main materials, brick and timber. The result could have been powerful but without life, if the stairs and gallery had not achieved a delight through the way the timber, the organ and its case have been handled. By comparison, the altar, altar rails, font and pulpit are disappointing, and show an arbitrariness in their design. In the building as a whole there is a living coherence which these parts lack.

◀ Danish Seamen's Church

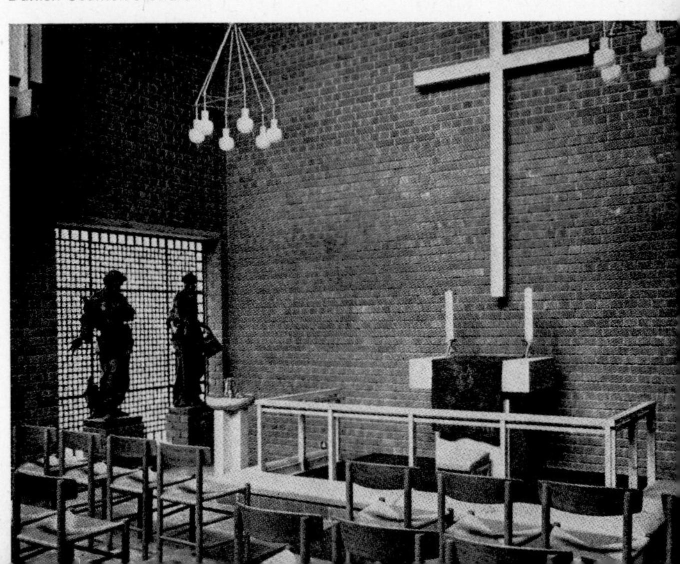

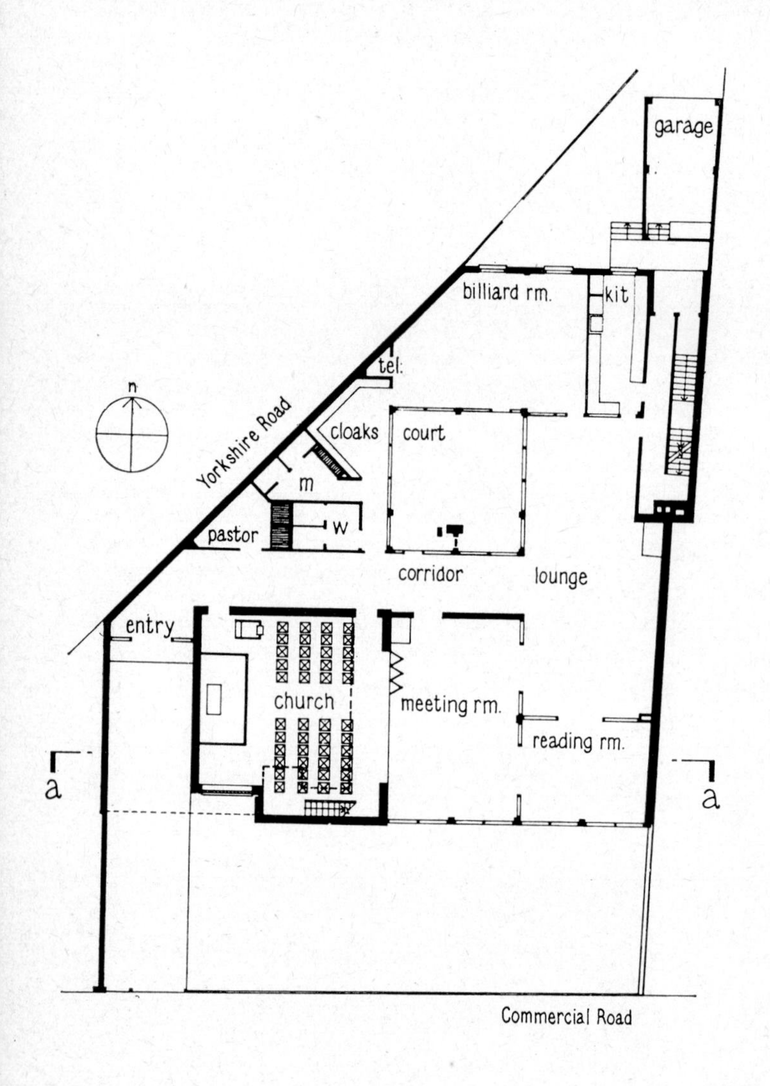

Danish Seamen's Church plan

Danish Seamen's Church

Gerhard Hauss and H. Richter
CHURCH OF THE DIASPORA Lutheran
ÖSTRINGEN · WEST GERMANY 1959

This little church, seating about 100 people, looks ordinary; yet in its way it is complete and satisfactory. The most obviously interesting thing about it is the brick sculpture—a kind of decoration very difficult to bring off. The architects have got away with it, because it is carefully controlled and part of the whole building, not something stuck on.

A very simple vernacular formula has been chosen and developed with great care, but the formula is so simple that any misjudgement in scale, proportion or detail could be fatal. At first sight, there is nothing strikingly 'modern' about the building, but the concrete, the roof structure and the glazing have been used in a way in which they would not have been used before. An instance of the kind of care which has gone into the building is the two diagonal braces in the corner windows, which strengthen the corners structurally and visually without disturbing the consistency and rhythm of the glazing.

Everywhere results have been achieved with great economy; at the entrance end of the church there is a concrete screen, which is glazed in the upper part to make a west window, and is open in the lower part between the church and the narthex. Throughout, there is delight in ordinary materials; for instance, in the design of the tower which is perfectly thought out for concrete, and again in the way that brickwork and concrete are related under the eaves. The stained glass in this little building—unlike that in so many new churches—is a perfect part of the design; it succeeds not only from inside but from outside as well, the delicacy of the leading setting off the power of the brick and concrete. The stained glass artist is clearly in contact with the architectural function of his art—a rare quality in stained glass, since the fourteenth century.

Church of the Diaspora

On another level, in spite of the simplicity of the church, its symbolic pattern is interesting. The form of the brick ship on the outside, for example, relates to the form of the church, thus giving a new dimension to the sculpture. The mast and spar make a cross on the outside, but this is not carried through to the inside because of the cross on the table. Very often today church towers are pointless formal essays or conjuring tricks, but at Östringen the way the tower has been used to emphasize the door is beautiful. The door, tower, bell and the three steps up to them together are powerful; there is a convincing economy about the arrangement. This relationship of door and tower is moving probably because it recalls an ancient symbolic pattern—the gate to the Heavenly City through a towered entrance. The low narthex through which you pass into the higher space of the church is also well calculated.

Church of the Diaspora

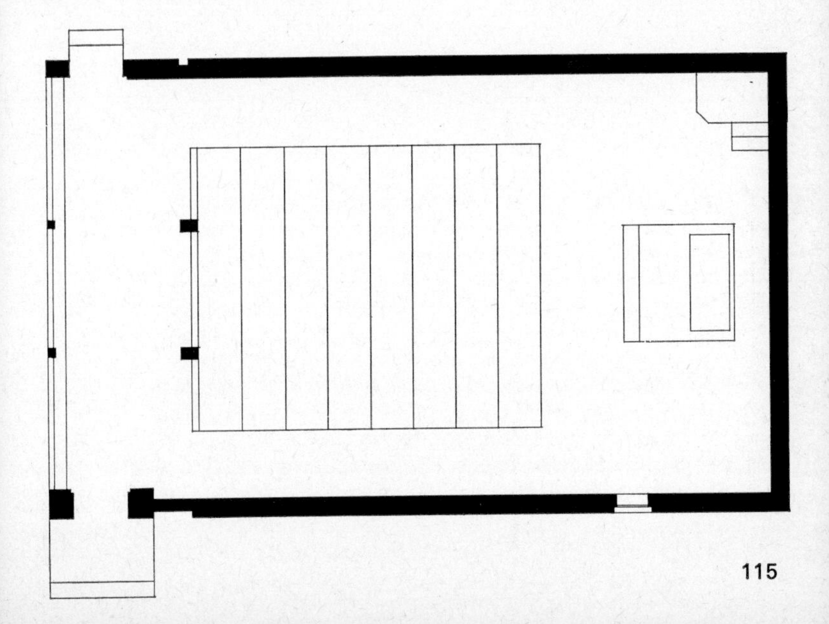

Rudolf Schwarz
ST CHRISTOPHORUS RC
COLOGNE-NIEHL · WEST GERMANY 1960

This is Schwarz's last completed church, built for a suburb of Cologne which was 'not very religious', so that the church serves a special missionary function. Schwarz wrote that he discarded about forty projects in order to arrive at a building in which all that is unnecessary has been excluded. This process could so easily have led to an over-refined perfectionism. In fact the building has a refinement that is free and intense—a vitality which is the result of a deep concern for the life of the Church, not for the perfection of architecture.

The church has an ordinary concrete frame with panels of common bricks; the windows, though filled with stained glass, are ordinary industrial metal windows. In comparison with these cheap materials the floor is rich, particularly in the marble around the font and in the sanctuary. Schwarz uses the floorscape as a most important element in the symbolic pattern of the church, relating the altar and the font to each other and to the space of the church.

Although the interior is not bright, it is light-filled. Some of the means by which this has been achieved can be identified. The light is picked up by the structure, columns and roof beams; it is reflected from the floor and caught by the lighting fittings. Yet the experience of light in the church goes beyond these. Very subtly and undramatically one is made aware of light as if the building contained it. The Eastern Church speaks of a church—through an analogy with the mother of God—as the 'container of the incontainable'. St Christophorus makes it possible to understand this.

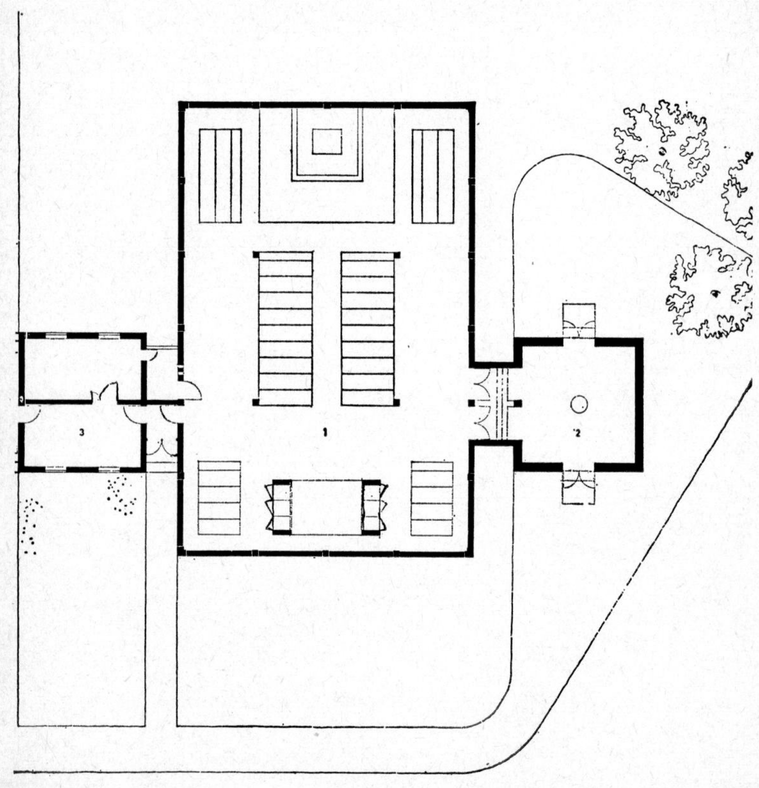

St Christophorus plan

St Christophorus

Richard Hughes
AFRICAN GIRLS' HIGH SCHOOL CHURCH Anglican
KIKUYU · KENYA 1959

The main structure of the chapel consists of short columns supporting clusters of struts that are made of creosoted telegraph poles; these support rafters which are also telegraph poles. Each rafter, with its struts, is held in position by the layer of boarding. The roof is independent of the side walls, being held down at the eaves with steel rods. The stone walls are only six inches thick and zigzagged for stability. The chapel seats 300 and cost under £3,000, which is very cheap even for Kenya. It is not just cheap: it has a true economy which goes beyond mere cheapness.

There is a great deal of space in the building; the use of an apse gives a large sanctuary without wasting floor area, there is ample room for movement as the seats do not extend beyond the line of the columns, and the form of the side wall gives a spaciousness beyond what is actually there.

The relationship of the congregation to the sanctuary, although orthodox in the sense that the seating is arranged in two blocks facing 'east', is modified by the form of the interior. The accent is on width rather than length, and the curved wall of the sanctuary embraces the space of the chapel while retaining the special character that sets it apart, yet not divided off. The columns and clusters of struts give the whole interior a distinctive quality—that of being a 'place'.

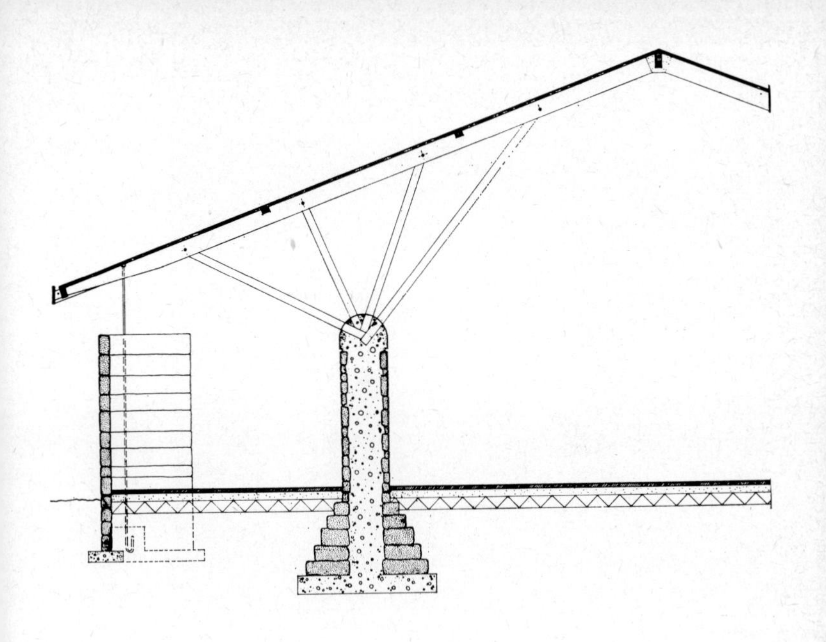

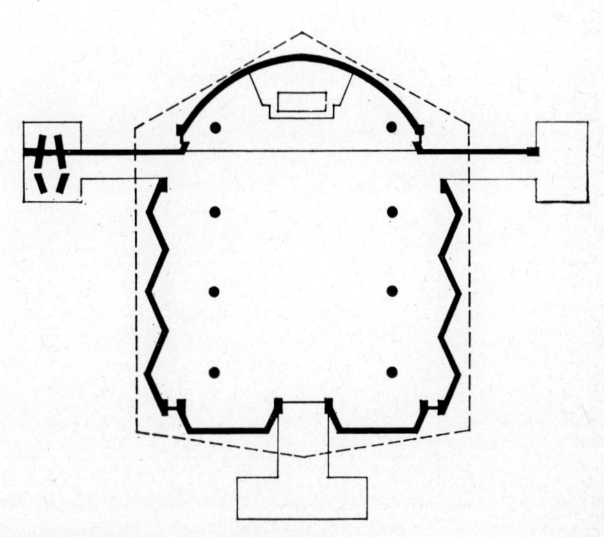

African Girls' High School plan and section

African Girls' High School

Wheeler and Sproson
ST COLUMBA Presbyterian
GLENROTHES · SCOTLAND 1960

The unity of the People of God in worship, particularly in the Eucharist, and an awareness of St Paul's teaching of the Church as the body of Christ, have been principal themes of the Liturgical Movement. Since the Reformation, the increasing emphasis on preaching among Presbyterians had led—until recently—to the domination of their churches by pulpits. The Lord's Supper and so the Holy Table had become relatively less important. The influence of the Liturgical Movement on the development of Presbyterian worship and architecture can be seen at Glenrothes. Although the pulpit still dominates the space it is not central in it, so that it is possible to develop other relationships in the building. The seating is arranged so that most of the people are gathered around three sides of the place of the Lord's Table. This is a development not only from the almost exclusive emphasis on the pulpit but also from the type of plan which provides a platform at one end of the building, as in the Presbyterian churches at Kent, Washington (p. 147) and East Liverpool, Ohio (p. 129).

At Glenrothes on 'Baptism Sundays', the table is replaced by the font so that baptism can take place 'in the face of the people'. The lantern and the four steel columns which support it unite the space of the building around the place of the Word, Baptism and Communion, setting it apart for worship. To quote the architects' theological brief: 'The church must be a preaching church such that the minister can be heard from all corners, yet the church is not primarily an auditorium; it is essentially a place set aside for worship'.

St Columba

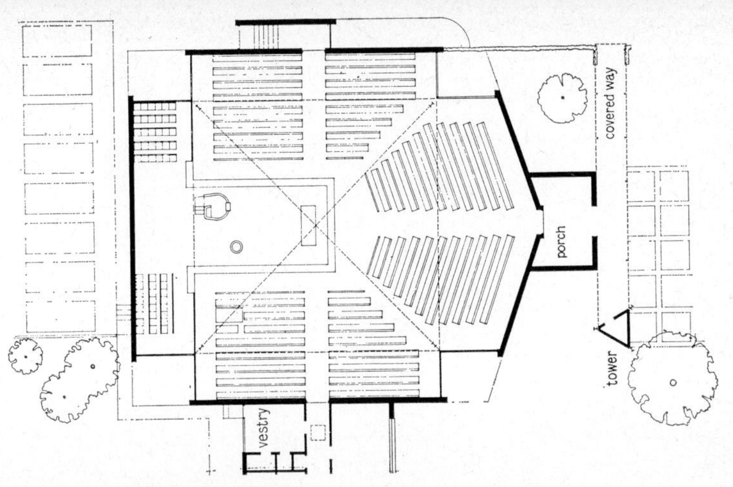

St Columba plan

Victor A. Lundy
FIRST UNITARIAN CHURCH Unitarian
WESTPORT, CONNECTICUT · U.S.A. 1960

This is a great timber roof supported on steel columns with a variety of accommodation arranged under it. The roof is made up of a solid deck of four-inch by two-inch timbers nailed together on to a powerful framework of curved laminated beams, which support and warp the deck; it is a very successful piece of timber engineering. Not only the timber structure is well handled, but also the steel frames which support it and the smaller details, like tubular spacers between the two wings of the roof. In most buildings in which the structure is used expressively, the effect is killed by the bodging which results from the fitting of a building into the structure. Lundy has avoided this by separating structure and accommodation with a plate glass infill; while this allows the structure to fulfil its own logic, it does not quite work, since, in spite of its transparency plate glass is solid.

Lundy has written 'the real sanctuary is the nature left there on the land'. This conception of a church is the opposite to a place set apart, but relates Lundy's design to the chapel at Otaniemi (p. 70) and also to Zen and other Far Eastern traditions, in which meditation is of central importance.

About churches in general, Lundy has said, 'I think the important question in church building, after all the intellectualizing, is *does it move you?*' This idea of an emotive form—architecture as sculpture—is widely held. Ronchamp (p. 48) is the most distinguished modern example. Often such an approach results in mere sentimentality. There are churches in the shape of praying hands, crowns of thorns or stained glass fish. The church at West Port is real sculpture not literary pseudo-symbolism, but it is still a private creation, apparently not a development from and for a living Christian community and tradition.

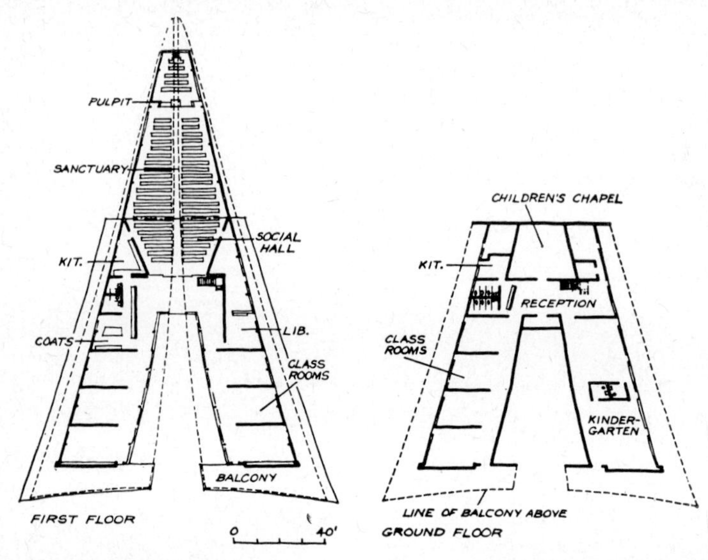

First Unitarian Church plan

Paul Schweikher
TRINITY PRESBYTERIAN CHURCH Presbyterian
EAST LIVERPOOL, OHIO · U.S.A. 1960

The planning of this building makes no great departure from the general run of American Protestant churches: a hall-type church with font, communion table, pulpit, choir and organ all arranged at the 'east' end; and a large wing containing the extensive *plant* (as it is unsentimentally termed): hall, meeting rooms, classrooms, lavatories, etc., all now regarded as essential to the work of the Church, and the subject of intensive planning. Schweikher's building has a formal clarity, however, which is unusual. But its main distinction is its structure and cladding: three kinds of concrete—*in situ*, precast and pressed blocks—form the whole building and are handled brilliantly in a primitive, stomping, Stonehenge way.

Inside, the contrast could not be greater, for the 'east' end furnishings are thin and slick and reminiscent of a boardroom or a hotel reception-hall. The communion table is a horizontal slab let into a long planting-box, with plants at each end; it almost irresistibly invites the placing of two white telephones upon it.

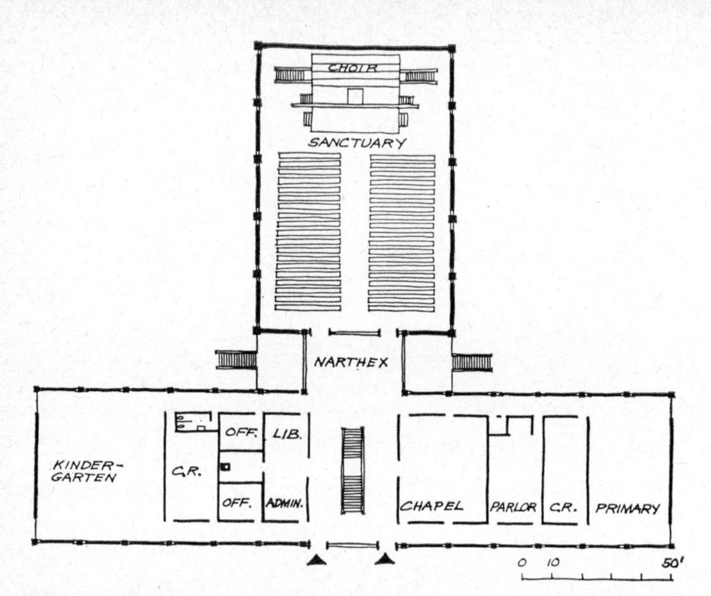

Trinity Presbyterian Church plan

Van den Broek and Bakema
CHURCH AT NAGELE Protestant
HOLLAND 1961

The new village of Nagele is a study in controlled enclosure on every scale. The village itself lies within an enclosing belt of forest, which shields it from the winds and from the infinity of the reclaimed polder. Neighbourhoods are arranged to look inwards on their own central spaces, with a release on one side towards the village centre. Each tradesman has a house, workshop and shop around a small courtyard, opened to the public place only by the large shop window. The church, by the same architects, increases in enclosure by degrees, from the open space of the village centre, through the courtyard and porch to the church space itself.

Materials and construction in the church, as in the rest of the village, are simple and within the scope of the local craftsmen who built it: concrete block, *in situ* and precast concrete, and timber, all used with a refreshing frankness.

The church is a simple rectangular room with precast concrete beams, heavily defined but well lit, so that the top-lighting above

the pulpit and communion table gives a feeling of lightening of touch rather than of high drama (compare the similar device but altogether different result at Farsta, p. 140). This lightening has allowed the architects to dispose the pulpit, communion table, font and organ with a freedom and balance which is remarkable in so small a space; it is successful, also, because the objects themselves are simplified to their *essential* characters, so that each stands clearly apart from the other, distinguished by its function (again, compare the same objects in the chapel at Otaniemi, where all are reduced to a least-common-denominator and so become inconsequential).

This is perhaps the simplest, and certainly one of the most successful, applications of the 'broad front' idea, in which the centres of liturgical action are spread out along one wall of the church. It suffers from the inevitable shortcoming of such an arrangement—that the rest of the church is spatially static and rigidly related to the liturgical centres; even though these may be dynamically related to each other.

Church at Nagele

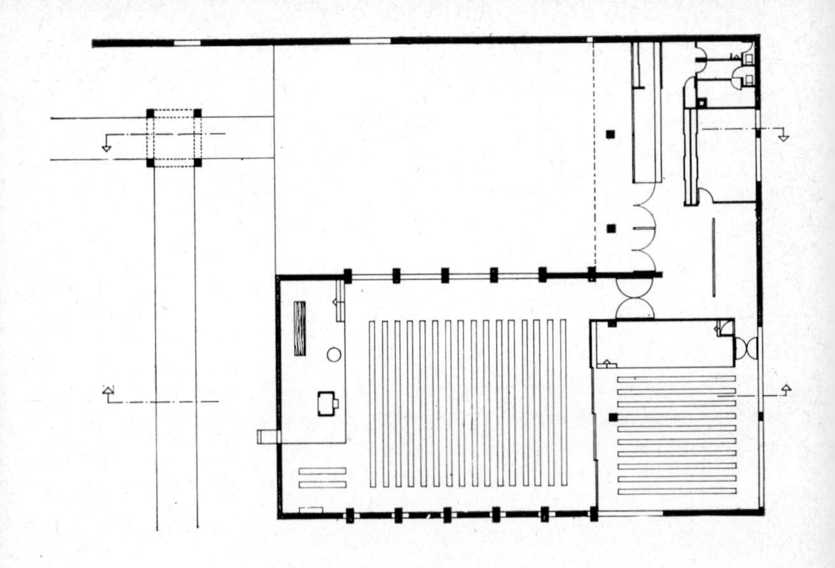

Church at Nagele

Alexander Von Branca
CHURCH AT ROHRBACH RC
WEST GERMANY 1961

This group of buildings in the middle of a cabbage field gives a feeling of warmth and friendliness; yet it is not sentimental, cosy, or sweet. The attraction of the group is partly that the buildings seem to grow out of the landscape like a good farm and partly the way the materials have been used.

Inside, the materials are rugged without being crude. The tough timber roof is traditional in technique but a modern structure; such integration of traditional and modern is perfectly natural in the countryside, where traditional skills still exist. The relationship between the brick and concrete of the floor, like the relationship of the plaster and concrete of the exterior, is beautiful.

The font is in a baptistery at the base of the tower; you look down into it from the entrance cloister.

The plan is like that of the Steel Church (p. 18)—a slightly tapered rectangle and apse. The way the structure above the altar breaks the swing of the apsidal wall behind the altar is disturbing because otherwise the church is taut and coherent. The square-columned structure not only disrupts the integrity of the clerestory wall but also breaks the rhythm of the circular columns and

crashes into the roof structure. But though this structure is untidy, it does something for the symbolic pattern of the church, giving the building a depth which distinguishes it from most new churches. The function of square columns and the high space above the altar is to define the altar space, distinguishing it within the space of the church. In this they act like the columns at St Albert, Saarbrüken (p. 66) or the corona and ciborium at St Paul, Bow Common (p. 90). There is no sense of exclusion, because the altar space is tied into the space of the church by the strong enclosing wall which sets apart and unites all the space within it. Von Branca's building has affinities with the unified but differentiated space of an Orthodox church, rather than the two spaces—chancel and nave—of a western medieval church.

The whole interior and the things in it give the impression that it has been designed out of a deep feeling for liturgy. The celebrants' seat behind the altar, and the reading place to one side of it, have the conviction of things made for a purpose which is profoundly understood.

Church at Rohrbach

Church at Rohrbach

Church at Rohrbach plan

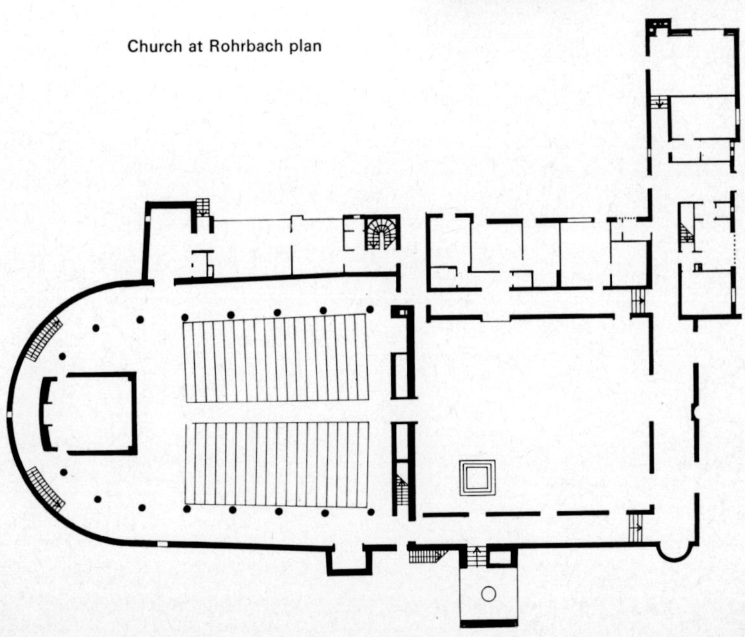

Hans Borgström and Bengt Lindroos
CHURCH AT FARSTA Lutheran
NEAR STOCKHOLM · SWEDEN 1961

This group of buildings, near the main centre of a new town, includes a large number of rooms for social purposes as well as the church itself—a consequence, partly, of the position of the established Church in Sweden. Perhaps it is this also which is reflected in the relationship of the buildings to the surrounding landscape; they are self-assured, almost aggressive in their command of the area around. The church is romantic in the castle-fortress manner, with clear-cut cubic masses rising high, a silhouette of great bells against the sky, earth piled up against the walls or cut away to reveal a great arch, entrance to the mortuary. All this is carried out in a masterly way, in dark-brown brick, concrete left from the mould and pine.

The interior of the church borders on the theatrical. Fundamentally its plan is traditional, but the traditional static relationships between altar and people, pulpit and people, are played up—over-emphasized by the height, the relentless drive of the massive side-walls, and the light from the unseen source above the altar. The effect is again masterly, but stops short at being an effect pure and simple; the form of worship imposed is no less rigid for its dramatic setting.

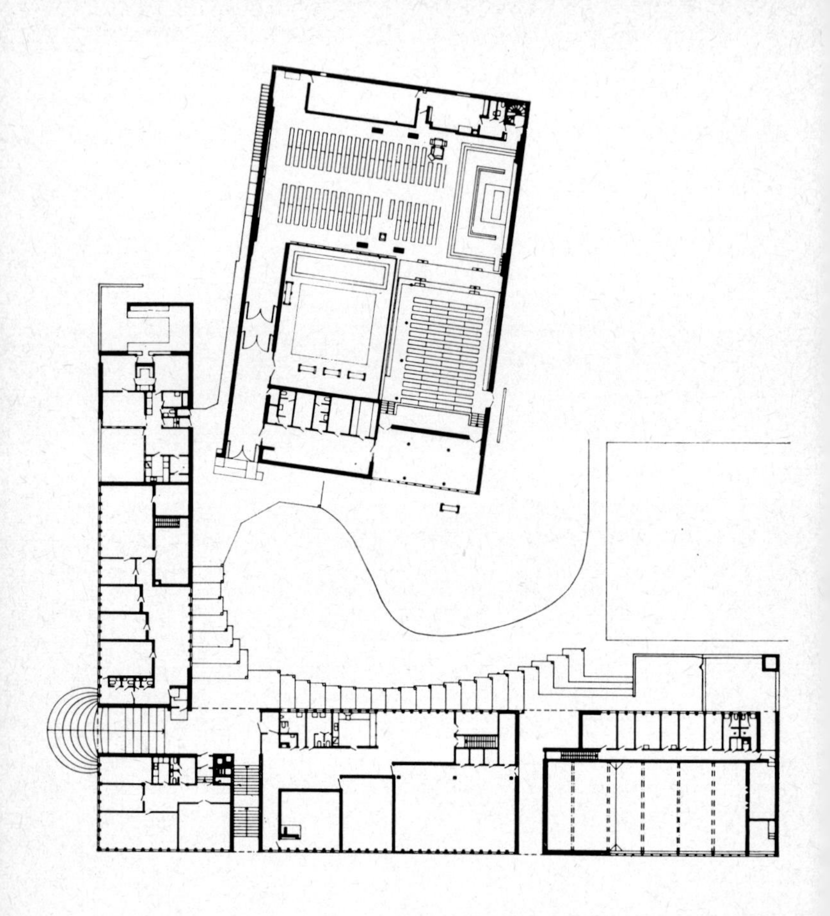

Church at Farsta plan

The church excludes the outside world and has that quality of 'placeness' which makes it a sanctuary in the broader sense. The interior does not rely, as is a tendency in Scandinavian churches, upon a view of the world of nature to sustain itself (compare the chapel at Otaniemi, p. 70, where the pine-trees outside, in juxtaposition to the cross, are made objects of contemplation). Seen in this context, the sculpted figures on the wall above the altar gain in significance, because they are arranged as the true culmination of the interior. Their fastidious realism is disturbing, particularly since they are slightly smaller than life-size. They are like small but real people who have climbed out along the ledge; and one is led to wonder what purpose they serve, and whether it has more than a superficial relationship to Christianity.

Church at Farsta

Gillespie, Kidd and Coia
ST MARY OF THE ANGELS RC
CAMELON · SCOTLAND 1961

This is a complicated little building on a simple plan. It has kick, chiefly because of its timber structure. The main roof timbers, at two levels, lock into timber columns, which divide the aisle from the nave. At their outside ends the roof beams are supported directly by the walls; above the walls, between the beams, are windows. This is all quite straightforward and convincing. The basic simplicity has been jazzed-up with complicated day-lighting; flues in the roof (which look as though they derive from La Tourette, p. 52), a strip of light above the aisle, a break in the walls. In the same way the brickwork is full of nooks and crannies. It is interesting to compare the brickwork here with the brickwork of the church at Östringen (p. 112), which looks as if it was conceived in brick: this building looks as if it had been designed in some other material—say concrete—and then built in brick.

The plan and seating is rigid, and there are two altars and two tabernacles. This shows a typically British lack of liturgical sense. So far, in spite of considerable interest in liturgical reform, the feeling for liturgy which has developed among Roman Catholics in the countries bordering the Rhine has not yet gone very deep in Britain. In fact, the Liturgical Movement has not had the form-giving power which is so impressive in the best continental churches. To a great extent churchbuilding in Britain gives the impression of a transitional period, in which the style and shape of churches is changing only as a result of influences from outside, not as a result of inner changes in the Church.

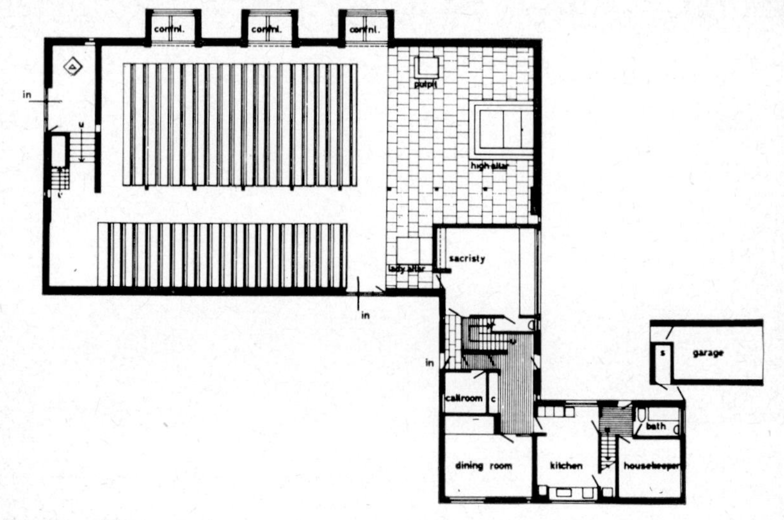

St Mary of the Angels plan

St Mary of the Angels

Durham, Anderson and Freed
FIRST PRESBYTERIAN CHURCH Presbyterian
KENT, WASHINGTON · U.S.A. 1962

The scale of church-building activity is greater in the United States than anywhere else, and unfortunately the growth of understanding of the nature and purpose of churches has fallen far short of the rate of expansion. Recently, however, a small number of churchmen and architects, aware of the dangers of the situation, have led a movement for more informed design; and, because of a pragmatic approach which avoids setting the sights too high and aims at wide dissemination of ideas, their success is recorded in a large number of intimate, simple churches in which the grandiose is rejected. The First Presbyterian Church at Kent illustrates the achievement in a formula which is successful because of the deliberate use of domestic scale and materials.

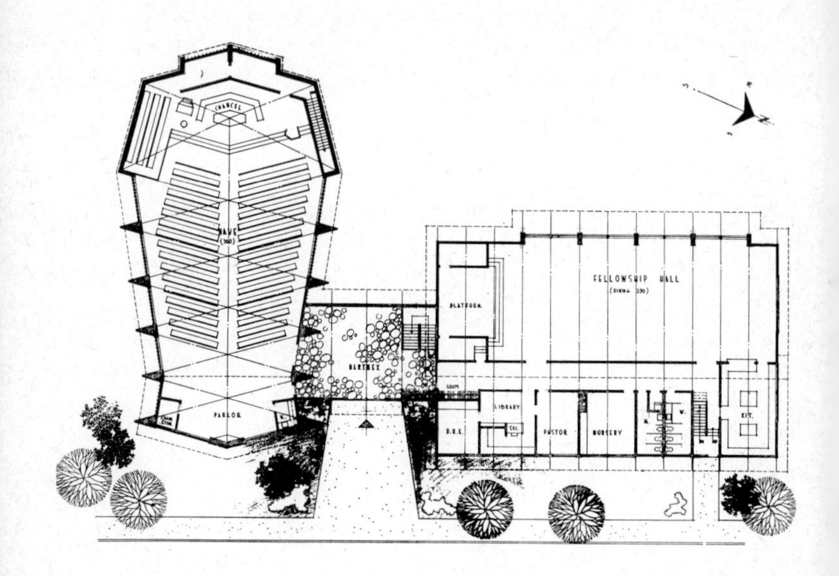

First Presbyterian Church plan

First Presbyterian Church

Emil Steffan
ST LAURENTIUS RC
LINDENTHAL, COLOGNE · WEST GERMANY 1962

This is a plainish brick box standing on a street corner in the university area of Cologne. The cubic form is strong, but weakened by folksy brickwork; in contrast the organ loft, made of undisguised concrete, is refreshingly straightforward. Inside, the space of the organ loft and the beautiful spiral stair up to it lighten what would otherwise be a rather sombre building.

The spiral stair is a remarkable work. The manner in which it rises from the powerful stone pad around a circular pole like a stripped tree trunk, the spring of the laminated timber string, and the coherence of the whole seem to be the consequence of a strong feeling for the idea of a stair, which goes beyond the practical need to get up into the loft. Ladders and stairs have had a symbolic meaning in many ancient cultures and among primitive peoples. They are part of a group of related symbols communicating aspiration, ascension, the movement between different planes of reality: like the ladder in Jacob's dream. Mircea Eliade writes in *Images and Symbols* 'The ideas of sanctification, of death, love and deliverance are all involved in the symbolism of the stair. . . . But it must not be forgotten that the staircase symbolizes these things because it is thought to be set up in a "centre", because it makes communication possible between different levels of being.'

It is unlikely that Steffan was explicitly conscious of any of these ideas when he was designing the stair; but the result has a presence which distinguishes it from most objects designed for churches today, a quality which relates it to primitive ritual things and speaks to the deep levels of consciousness which Eliade writes about.

The plan of the seating, and the slight raking of the floor down to the altar-place, occur also in the same architect's St Laurentius at Munich (p. 78); but the idea works less well here because there is no space behind the altar and because the altar-place is comparatively pedestrian.

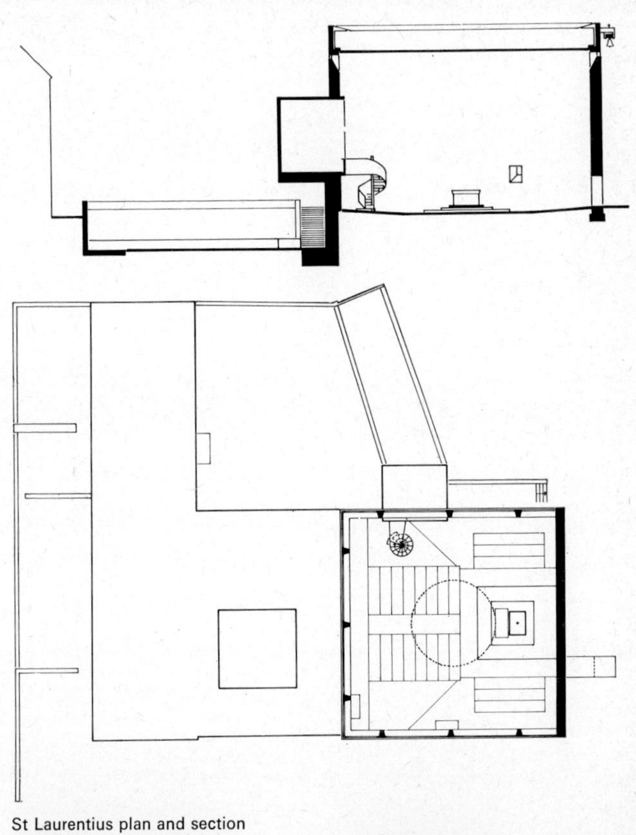

St Laurentius plan and section

Denis Aubert
CHURCH OF THE RECONCILIATION Reformed and RC
TAIZÉ · FRANCE 1962

Taizé is one of the small number of protestant religious communities, and the architect of the church is a member of the community. To begin with, the community was lent a little medieval church; and the new church has been built to accommodate the tradition of worship which had grown up in this. The community is dedicated to Ecumenical prayer. There is a Roman Catholic chapel in the crypt of the new church. Besides its close contacts with Roman Catholics the Taizé Community has been specially influenced by Orthodox communities in France. This Ecumenical openness can be felt in the design of the church.

The building is on the edge of a hill, cut into the earth like an amphitheatre. The narthex is slightly distinguished from the choir and sanctuary by being on a higher level, so that it is not quite within the 'place' of the church, which is the area within the steps. From the narthex those who are interested in, but not yet committed to, the worship can see and hear, and to that extent take part in the worship of the Church.

The altar is on steps above the floor of the nave and in a slightly separated altar-place. Apart from two narrow slit windows in the side walls it is lit from above. The steps up to the altar, the lighting and the spatial distinction of the altar-place from the rest of the church make the relationship between altar-place and church like that between an apron stage and auditorium. Even so it isn't cut off from the rest of the space of the building, because the concrete grid of the main roof structure is carried through underneath the roof of the altar space, so that the triangular coffers are lit from above. This device links the two parts firmly together.

As the church is a pilgrimage place, the steps make more room for people to stand. The choir is small and intimately related to the altar. The seats are without kneelers ; the brethren are open to each other, and this encourages a greater unity than a traditional choir with choir stalls.

The logic of the design is partly a consequence of the roof structure, which, based on equilateral triangles, results in sixty-degree internal angles rather than right angles. This formula is difficult to handle, particularly if there are also squares on plan.

From the outside this church in a field has a practical look : the architect has been interested in designing for his community, not in impressing other people.

Church of the Reconciliation

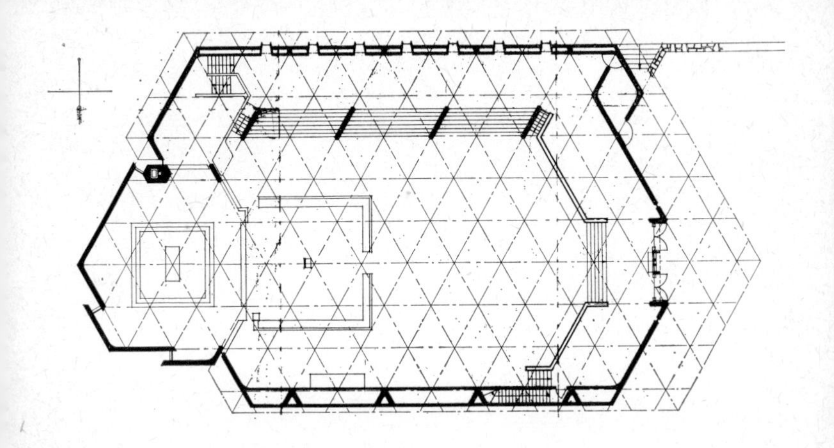

Church of the Reconciliation plan

Church of the Reconciliation

Index

Architects

Church Names

Place Names

Bibliography

Guide to Modern Architecture by Reyner Banham
Architectural Press, London, 1962

Theory and Design in the First Machine Age by Reyner Banham
Architectural Press, London, 1960

Towards a Church Architecture edited by Peter Hammond
Architectural Press, London, 1962

Liturgy and Architecture by Peter Hammond
Barrie & Rockliff, London, 1960

This Before Architecture by Edward S. Frey
Foundation Books, Jenkintown Pennsylvania, 1963

Life and Liturgy by Louis Bouyer
Sheed and Ward, London, 1956

Liturgy and Society by A. G. Hebert
Faber and Faber, London, 1935

Spirit of the Liturgy by Romano Guardini
Sheed and Ward, London, 1930

Christianity and Symbolism by F. W. Dillistone
Collins, London, 1955

Patterns in Comparative Religion by Mircea Eliade
Sheed and Ward, London, 1958

Sacred and Profane Beauty: the Holy in Art by Geradus Van der Leeuw
Weidenfeld & Nicolson, London, 1963

Dominikus Böhm, a monograph
Verlag Schnell und Steiner, Munich, 1962

Kirchenbau by Rudolf Schwarz
F. H. Kerle Verlag, Heidelberg, 1960

The Church Incarnate: the Sacred Nature of Christian Architecture by Rudolf Schwarz, trans. Cynthia Harris, Henry Regnery Co., Chicago, 1958

Der Baumeister Otto Bartning und die Wieder-Entdeckung des Raumes by Hans K. F. Mayer, Lambert Schneider, Heidelberg, 1951